WITH RUCKSACK AND BUS PASS

Walking the Thames Path

BY THE SAME AUTHOR

'Julie'
a novel

WITH RUCKSACK AND BUS PASS

Walking the Thames Path

Beverley Hansford

Matador
5 Weir Road
Kibworth Beauchamp
Leicester LE8 0LQ, UK
Tel: (+44) 116 279 2299
Fax: (+44) 116 279 2277
Email: books@troubador.co.uk
Web: www.troubador.co.uk/matador

ISBN 978 1848765 375

British Library Cataloguing in Publication Data.
A catalogue record for this book is available from the British Library.

Edited by Helen Banks

While every care has been observed in the preparation of this book and the information it contains, no
responsibility or liability can be accepted for any errors which may have inadvertently been
incorporated

Typeset in 12pt Palatino by Troubador Publishing Ltd, Leicester, UK

Matador is an imprint of Troubador Publishing Ltd

Printed in Great Britain by the MPG Books Group, Bodmin and King's Lynn

*To the people who have already experienced the
joy of walking the length of the Thames Path,
and to those who still have that pleasure to come.*

Contents

Prelude

How it all began…

Neither my wife, Johanna, nor I can remember where the idea originally came from. It may have been reading something somewhere, or purchasing a guidebook to the Thames Path walk which remained on the bookshelf unread for several years. Either way, the thought remained just 'a good idea sometime'. It was when we heard about two retired people actually walking the length of the Thames Path that the idea started to flourish. Soon it became a case of not 'Should we do it?' but 'When shall we do it?'

With no holiday plans in place, we decided that 2009 would be an excellent year to undertake the project, and planning started. It has to be said that once a decision had been made some doubts did start to emerge. We asked ourselves whether two people in their seventies would be able to sustain the distances involved. The guidebooks talked calmly of walking sections of 10 or 12 miles – even 16 miles. True, we maintained a healthy lifestyle and had a large allotment to cultivate, which kept us reasonably fit, but we had never walked the distances involved: our walking had been of the five-or-six-mile variety and that not on a regular basis.

We decided to test our stamina by walking one of the shortest stretches close at hand. We felt ourselves quite fortunate that we lived roughly halfway along the Thames Path and only about 5 miles from the nearest point. We considered that Henley-on-Thames to Marlow at around 8 miles would be a suitable test. One frosty January morning we set off by bus to Henley. We had already decided that if we did do the Thames Path walk it would be completed using public transport whenever possible. By the time we arrived in Henley the sun was already brightening up the cool morning. After a coffee in the town to boost our confidence, we ventured forth.

This particular section of the Thames Path proved to be a good trial run. The route follows the river nearly all the way, except for one small section when it is necessary to make a detour inland and walk on land overlooking the river; but this is not an unpleasant diversion – unlike some we were to encounter later on. This was also our first experience of following the walking instructions from a guidebook. We had purchased David Sharp's excellent book *The Thames Path* and I would earnestly recommend this guide to anyone contemplating the walk. The book is divided into convenient sections and contains detailed bit-by-bit instructions together with maps and photographs. It is part of the National Trail Guides series and is an invaluable companion. For walkers looking for overnight accommodation the *Thames Path National Trail Companion* published by The National Trails Office is a useful addition. We found it useful to have a plastic cover for a guidebook or map for protection from damage and from the occasional rain shower.

As we walked our 'test piece', the winter sun gathered strength. The white frost covering everything started to disappear and with it the morning chill. Unfortunately, some areas of the ground which had hitherto been frozen solid started to thaw out and it became a bit muddy underfoot, but this was a minor distraction. After we left behind Henley, the few joggers out early and the occasional person being taken out by a dog for a walk, contact with other human beings became less frequent; not until we reached Hambleden Lock with its picturesque view of Hambleden Mill, some 2 miles from the start, did we see several people enjoying the tranquillity. This is the point at which the walk leaves the Thames for a quarter of a mile or so, and after that we had the river to ourselves until we approached Marlow. Water birds continued to do their own thing, ignoring our presence, and the cows we passed looked up from their grazing to study the intruders, questioning why their peace had been disturbed.

We walked on steadily, sometimes in conversation, sometimes in silence, intent on achieving our goal. When Danesfield House Hotel came into view perched high on the opposite bank, we knew we were well past halfway, and by the time Hurley Lock appeared, we were confident of success. Nevertheless, the sight of the steeple of Marlow church was a welcome one. By now the track alongside the river had become a sticky mess of mud in the early afternoon sun. At times it was necessary to walk on the grass fringe to avoid slipping in the mire. The pleasant winter afternoon had brought the residents of Marlow out to take an afternoon walk along the river. Young families and dog walkers were in abundance.

We arrived in Marlow, glad that our exercise was completed but also feeling well satisfied that we had achieved what we had started out to do. We had finished the task we had set ourselves and had walked at a steady 2½ miles per hour. Not bad, we thought, for two pensioners. Our confidence had been primed to look forward to greater things.

Kemble To Cricklade

12.4 MILES (19.8 KILOMETRES)

For several weeks after our trial run weather conditions were not favourable for walking and it was not until March that we were able to return to any serious thoughts of commencing the Thames Path walk proper. Even then one disturbing aspect of the project started to worry us. There had been quite a lot of rain in the preceding weeks and our thoughts turned to what the walking conditions would be like around the area of the source. Various photographs we looked at showed it to be flooded with water at times. What would it be like after the recent wet weather? A telephone call to the National Trails Office only reinforced our concerns. In the end it was Johanna who came up with a solution. We were due to make one of our occasional trips to an organic farm shop in the area. Why not, she suggested, include a visit to the source and take wellington boots as a precaution? It seemed to me to be an excellent idea, because neither of us really wanted to walk a long distance in wellington boots, or for that matter carry them all day in case we needed them, and on this occasion we would be no more than about 4 miles from the source.

The official source of the Thames is about a mile or so from the village of Kemble in Gloucestershire. Thames Path walkers have to make their way up to the source and then return to their starting point close to Kemble to continue their journey.

Saturday the 14th of March was the date chosen for our introduction to the Thames Path. The weather forecast was for white cloud with drizzle. At 7.45 a.m., as we set out along the M40 to Oxford, linking with the A40 and then branching off on the A429 towards Cirencester, the forecast was proving to be accurate. A leaden sky was producing a kind of dampness in the air. But the weather was a great deal better than it had been for the past few days. At least it was not raining.

Arriving at Abbey Home Farm, we indulged in a coffee in the farm shop restaurant to refresh ourselves before driving the remaining 4 miles to Kemble. Kemble is not very large, but it has a rail link to London. Once upon a time it was an important railway junction, with branch lines to Cirencester and Tetbury. Alas, the Tetbury branch suffered closure in 1963 followed by the Cirencester line in 1965. Today Kemble station has quite a sleepy air about it on a Saturday, but it is still an important link, as it is the nearest station to Cirencester. It was an essential part of our strategy for the current sortie. The railway information indicated that it had a car park, and this would be an integral part of our plan, because it is no more than a few hundred yards from the Thames Path.

It was mid-morning when we drove into Kemble and then down a rather narrow road with parked cars to the railway station. It proved to be a good decision. On a Saturday morning the large car park was almost empty and we thought the parking charge of £1.40 was extremely reasonable. As soon as we had parked the car, it was a quick change into wellington boots and then we were on our way.

Walking out of the station and then crossing the road led us to a stile, with the path clearly indicated across a field. Following the direction in which it pointed brought us to a wooden bridge over a shallow and sleepy stream no more than a few feet wide. This was what we had come to see: the infant Thames. The guidebook told us that we should cross the bridge and of course follow the flow of the water. We were pleased to experience quite fine weather in spite of the forecast.

The sky was overcast but there were signs of the clouds breaking and certainly no drizzle.

We ambled over the grass, with only a few water birds for company at first. Then we were surprised to see another walker heading towards us. It turned out to be Ron, who had also started his Thames Path walk that day. We chatted for several minutes and he insisted on taking a photograph of us. As we talked we were joined by another person, also on the same route. We were all quite surprised by the coincidence of all starting the walk and meeting at the same time. After this short break we pressed on. Within minutes the Thames veered away to the right into some trees. This appeared to be the spot where it makes its first appearance. In spite of the temptation to explore the area, we followed the instructions in the guidebook and continued across a wide field until we reached a farm track. Here the route was well marked, with instructions to walk across another large field to a stile. It was at this point that we made our first mistake. Seeing a stile ahead in the corner of the field, we made our way to it and found ourselves next to the A433, part of the Roman Lincoln-to-Exeter Fosse Way. This is a busy and fast stretch and great care was needed to cross as the instructions indicated. Unfortunately, on the other side we were faced by a thicket of tangled undergrowth. Definitely not the Thames Path, we decided. As we retraced our steps we spied a 4x4 dropping off a couple who looked as if they were on the same mission as we were. They headed for a point further down the road. A quick word with the driver confirmed our assumption that we had left the field at the wrong spot and that the actual route lay just down the road where the couple were heading. What we learned on the return trip was that there are two stile exits from the field. We had chosen the wrong one, partly as a result of not reading the guidebook correctly. Subdued and deflated by our early deficiency in navigation, we resumed the correct route, following the other couple, who walked in front of us across several fields dotted with trees. The source suddenly appeared ahead of us, almost concealed behind vegetation. To many people, particularly those who have walked the opposite route from the Barrier to the source, the actual spot might be rather an anticlimax. No water is gushing out from deep down; just a simple stone marking the spot. Having seen pictures of the area flooded, we were surprised to find that the ground underfoot was completely dry, in spite of recent rain; our wellington boots had been an unnecessary addition. We had now caught up with the two walkers we had followed from the A433. They turned out to have come from the Isle of Man, intent on spending the next fourteen days walking the Thames Path. We chatted for a few minutes and sealed the occasion and the start of both our enterprises by taking snapshots of each other. During our own walk over the next few months, we often thought of that couple and wondered if they had succeeded in their quest. It was quite a surprise on that quiet Saturday morning in March, on the first hour of our journey, to meet four other individuals all starting on the same expedition as we were and all walking in the same direction. It was a coincidence that was never repeated during the entire length of our journey of 184 miles. We met many Thames Path walkers, but all were travelling in the opposite direction. However, as Johanna pointed out, anyone who was walking in the same direction as we were would either be in front or behind us. Nevertheless, we did find it strange that so many people chose to walk in the opposite direction, because for us part of the joy of walking this path is to see the river becoming larger and larger and the scenery changing as it makes its way to the sea.

With the source of the great river discovered and our objective for the day completed, we retraced our steps to Kemble, enjoying the spring sunshine that now lit up our surroundings. Back at the car, we changed our completely dry footwear and drove back to Abbey Home Farm, where we enjoyed a late lunch. It had been a satisfying start to our journey.

The following Saturday we resumed our undertaking. It meant an early start, as this time we would be travelling by train to Kemble. First an early morning local train to Marylebone and then a quick change to Paddington, where we caught the 8.15 to Kemble. We had learnt the necessity of purchasing the tickets in advance if we were travelling very early. For one thing, most ticket offices are not open for the first trains, and for another, it does give that extra bit of time to make deadlines. On this occasion it enabled us to have a more leisurely approach and even have a cup of coffee at the Costa store before boarding the train at Paddington. We were fortunate to discover that our train was headed for Cheltenham Spa, stopping at Kemble, eliminating the normal requirement to change at Swindon.

It was almost half past nine when the train pulled into Kemble station. With the familiarity gained from the previous week, we quickly retraced our steps to where our last walk had ended. The weather forecast was for a fine sunny day and as we resumed our walk, even at that time in the morning it felt almost like a May or June day instead of March.

A short walk brought us to the bridge where we would take up the route again. As we left the road to walk alongside the infant Thames, two horse riders joined us. We held the gate leading off the road for them and they greeted us with a cheery 'Good morning'. We were all going the same way, but with their horse power they soon left us behind and disappeared from our sight. We were walking through pleasant fields, the Thames scarcely more than a stream flowing quite slowly and quietly alongside us, at times almost hidden by undergrowth. Eventually the walk over the fields ended at a road; the Thames disappeared from view and the guidebook instructed us to turn left down the road into the village of Ewen. The road proved to be quiet, with little traffic, and a few minutes' walk brought us into the small village. Quite a few residents busy about their morning tasks greeted us in a friendly manner and two ladies asked us where we were walking to. We confidently told them that we were on the Thames Path walk and intended to reach Cricklade that day but hoped eventually to walk all the way to the Barrier in the Thames Estuary. They did not seem in the least surprised and wished us success on our mission. As we went on our way, I could not help thinking that they had probably greeted many other walkers intent on the same task, and despite our confident air so early in the journey, it did occur to me that over 180 miles lay ahead of us.

Just outside the village we joined up with the Thames again. Somehow it had circled round the village, finding its own route through the farmland. We left the track we were on and resumed the route beside the river, which meandered through the countryside. We kept up a steady pace, conscious that there was still a long way to go, but at the same time enjoying the experience of being in the countryside and appreciating the peace and tranquillity. For the most part, in these early stages it is possible to walk for miles out in the countryside with only birds for company. Mallards and waterhens were numerous and we saw one female swan sitting on her nest, calmly dozing away the time, while the male paddled silently a short distance away, concentrating on his foraging but with a watchful eye on the nest all the time. Johanna spent a few minutes capturing the scene with her camera.

At one point we passed close by the village of Somerford Keynes, just visible across the fields, with a footpath leading to it should any Thames Path walker be tempted to explore it further or require refreshment.

We continued our walk, enjoying the tranquillity of the countryside around us. However, this was interrupted by the route ending abruptly at a road. Here the guidebook instructions were to follow the road for a short distance to another, quite busy road. The Thames Path sign, which we were now becoming familiar with, confirmed that we had to follow this road for a short section. Walking on the verge brought us to a road that led to Neigh Bridge Country Park and Cotswold Water Park. This is an area of lakes made up from old gravel pits. It is a popular spot and on the day we were there quite a lot of parents were in evidence, taking their children out for the day and enjoying being in the fresh air. It also seemed to be good for fishing, judging by the numerous anglers who lined the water's edge here and there.

For about an hour we walked along rather pleasant tree-lined paths. We did go wrong at one stage. Instead of turning sharp left as we should have done, we continued along the main path beside one of the lakes, interrupting the fishermen in their solitude. After about six or seven minutes we realised our error and retraced our steps to pick up the Thames Path again. Though this was the second time we had gone wrong so far, in fairness it had to be said that our mistake was an easy one to make. The sharp turn required is not very well marked. Oddly, from that point on we had little difficulty in finding the correct route, which, providing one has a good guidebook, is on the whole well marked and fairly easy to follow.

It was just after midday when we arrived at the slightly larger village of Ashton Keynes, which is recorded in the Domesday Book, though under a different name. It has changed its name a number of times throughout its history. It is usually considered that Ashton means a 'homestead with ash trees', while the second half of the name is derived from the Keynes family, who can trace their ancestry back to Norman times. It is recorded that the family were lords of the manor in the area as far back as the 13th century. The village is known for its four ancient crosses, and the church is appropriately called Holy Cross. The village provided a welcome refreshment and comfort break for us after our morning's walk. The guidebook mentions the White Hart and we found it in the main street without difficulty. It turned out to be quite a pleasant village pub, with just a few locals sampling its wares at lunchtime. The friendly landlady, who served us at the bar, asked us where we had come from and where we were bound; when we replied 'Cricklade', she confirmed that it was about a five-mile walk. It was comforting to know that we were now over halfway on our day's journey. After a refreshing glass of cider and a twenty-minute stop, we were on our way again.

Ashton Keynes is a pleasant and convenient rural location in which to live, and our route took us along quiet roads lined with modern houses built in the traditional yellow Cotswold stone. Next we were obliged to cross over some playing fields to finally clear the village. No activity was taking place, but as we walked past the pavilion I could not help wondering what the cricketers must think of Thames Path walkers disturbing their game. Through a gate, and we found ourselves out in the countryside again. But this was not the lush countryside we had experienced earlier. The well-defined track led us through a network of pools formed from old gravel pits. We had parted from the Thames in Ashton Keynes, and now it seemed to be lost from our view, winding its way through the maze of lakes that surrounded us. Instead of walking beside the river as we had done in the morning, we were now surrounded by swampy ground with tall reeds and tangled undergrowth. Notices warned against leaving the path; this was not actually quicksand, but something like it.

For the next few miles we walked at a steady pace. Now and then we would pass local walkers out enjoying the warm spring afternoon. Birdwatchers were quite noticeable, as the bird population appeared to be in abundance in the wetlands that surrounded us. The path was easy to follow, though occasionally muddy in places due to the recent rain. Eventually we appeared to leave the wetlands and found ourselves on a rather muddy section of the path. The guidebook informed us that we were following the route of the old railway line to Cricklade. It was nearly two hours since we had left Ashton Keynes, and we were both becoming tired, though we did not mention it to each other. It was pleasant when the Thames suddenly made an appearance again. It was an indication that we were not far from our destination, particularly when we caught sight of the expanse of North Meadow, a notable nature reserve. Here the wild snake's-head fritillary can sometimes be found.

We walked a little more slowly now, following the Thames, with Cricklade in view and the spire of St Sampson's church dominating the skyline. Across more fields, and then the river disappeared again, wandering around the town on its own path. We skirted round the edge of houses and through a gate, and suddenly we were in North Wall, at the foot of Cricklade High Street. Cricklade is a bustling little Cotswold town that was well established in Saxon times and has the distinction of being the only town in Wiltshire on the banks of the Thames, and the first along from the source. It has been a crossing place on the river as far back as records exist, and it was used in Roman times to connect several nearby roads. We wandered up into the centre, tired but congratulating ourselves. We calculated that the distance we had travelled was well over 10 miles. It was now 2.15 p.m. Our journey had taken four and a quarter hours of actual walking time, which worked out at almost 2½ miles an hour, a creditable pace for two pensioners.

Once we were in Cricklade our immediate quest was to find the stop for the bus to Swindon, where we could pick up the train for home. Walking up the High Street among the Saturday afternoon shoppers, we were surprised to discover how busy the tiny town was and how many small shops there were. We noticed several hotels that would be of interest to Thames Path walkers seeking a night's accommodation, including the Red Lion, which we had read about in a Triodos Bank newsletter. This traditional pub, which dates back to the 1600s, is a fully independent house and is establishing a reputation for good local food and beers. We could not pass without venturing inside. Unfortunately, it was quite full, and with thoughts of a bus to catch we decided to postpone a leisurely visit until another occasion.

Once outside again, being strangers in a strange town, we asked a passer-by where the bus stop was and he promptly directed us to the top of the street. When we arrived at the stop, bus no. 53, about which I had carefully enquired, appeared to be non-existent. However, there did appear to be another bus to Swindon, no. 51. As we were looking at the timetable a lady came across the road and helpfully asked us where we wanted to go. A few minutes' chat revealed that the no. 53 bus did not run from that stop, but from another a little distance away. Our informant confirmed that the no. 51 ran every hour from the stop where we were standing to Swindon – and that we had just missed one. Two other valuable bits of information were that the bus station in Swindon was only a few minutes' walk from the railway station and that the White Hart Hotel, close by here in Cricklade, provided a good cup of coffee.

After thanking this kind lady we retreated to the hostelry she had recommended and partook of a welcome cup of coffee and a sit-down in a comfortable chair. Thirty minutes later, suitably refreshed, we returned to the bus stop. By now several locals were waiting there. The bus arrived bang on time, and in answer to our concerned query the driver assured us cheerfully that our bus passes were 'fine'. We settled back for the twenty-minute ride. It was just coming up to four o'clock when we arrived at Swindon's modern bus station. The enquiry office was open, so with future bus rides in mind we took the opportunity to collect several timetables. We asked the way to the railway station and discovered that it was indeed no more than a few minutes walk away. We just managed to catch the 16.05 to London and home. As we settled back into the comfortable seats, we felt pleased with our first big effort at walking the Thames Path. It had been a good start.

SECTION TWO

Cricklade To Lechlade

10.9 MILES (17.4 KILOMETRES)

With the success of the first leg behind us we looked forward with enthusiasm to section two of the journey. We were already beginning to realise what an important part the weather plays in such enterprises as walking the length of the Thames. From the start we had decided that there was little point in walking for miles and miles in rain just to say we had done so, and that unless reasonable weather conditions were forecast there was little point in setting out. Not only that, but we wanted to enjoy the experience as well and indulge our hobby of photography. It is possible to take interesting and good photographs in the rain, but dry conditions are more comfortable.

Saturday the 4th of April, the day chosen for walking the next section, was in some doubt even the day before. In spite of a week of springlike weather, the forecast for the weekend had been for heavy rain. On the Friday evening, however, this had changed to a prediction of light drizzle clearing away during the morning. With this in mind, we decided to go, carefully packing waterproof trousers in our rucksacks.

The journey to Cricklade meant another early-morning start, but this was of no consequence as we were both early risers from habit and necessity. At half past six we set out for the bus station to catch the

11

first bus to Reading and from there a train to Swindon to connect with the local bus to Cricklade. It appeared to be complicated, but in reality it was quite straightforward. The only problem we had encountered at the initial planning stage of walking the Thames Path using mainly public transport had been the fact that we would have to use mostly Saturdays for the project, because in order to commence the walks by a reasonable hour it is necessary to have an early start. This completely rules out the use of bus passes and senior railcards on weekdays, as they are not valid before 9.00 a.m. except at weekends, when they can be used at any time. As we walked to the bus station this particular Saturday, light rain was falling as anticipated, but we set out optimistic for improvement. We spent an hour or so travelling on the bus to Reading, watching the grey clouds overhead and the drizzle obscuring the view from the windows. When we arrived in Reading we were pleased to find that the bus stop was close to the railway station. One surprise was that even using our railcards the fare to Swindon cost more than £27. With memories of how a similar amount had carried us for many more miles the previous summer in Germany, we realised how expensive rail fares are in the UK. While on the train to Swindon, we had an early cup of coffee from our flask. It was very comforting to observe that the weather conditions were improving: the rain had ceased and already bits of blue sky were showing through. It was a good omen.

When we arrived in Swindon, we quickly made our way to the bus station. A cool breeze circulated around the bus shelters, and with over half an hour to wait for the bus, we retreated to the nearby Octagon Café for another coffee. As it turned out this proved to be a good strategy, because the no. 51 bus was slightly late. However, within a few minutes of its arrival we were on our way to Cricklade, now a familiar route. It was pleasant to arrive in the sunshine, the grey clouds now quickly dispersing.

At this time on a Saturday morning the town was quiet, so we took the opportunity to take one or two photographs without the inconvenience of too many people or cars getting in the way. At the bottom of the High Street we picked up the Thames Path by turning into another street with the rather grand title of Abingdon Court Lane. Once away from the town, we were soon walking across meadows, with the steeple of St Sampson's church merging into the horizon. It did not take long before the Thames made an appearance. We followed the way it led, exchanging greetings with the few people we encountered: at this time of day these were mostly joggers or dog walkers. The guidebook explains that hereabouts the Thames is fed by the Churn, the Key and the Ray, which make it appear a more substantial river, though at this point it is still not big enough to support any river traffic. Walking under the A419 brought us out into more rural farmland. Soon we came to Eysey Footbridge, the first bridge over the Thames, which we had to cross to walk on the other side of the river. There are several footbridges on this section, but all the time the walk is through remote and peaceful farmland. Only here and there the footbridge indicated a link to some form of habitation. For the most part we had the Thames to ourselves with only the waterbirds for company: herons, moorhens and the occasional pair of swans.

One and a half hours of walking brought us to the village of Castle Eaton. Here again the Thames finds its own way past the village, leaving the walker to do the same. We had planned to have a break here and some form of refreshment in The Red Lion, a Georgian inn that has the distinction of being the first of many pubs along the route of the Thames. Unfortunately we arrived too early, and with almost an hour to wait until opening time we decided to press on. Castle Eaton has a church dedicated to St Mary the Virgin. Parts of it date back to Norman times, and it is perched almost on the banks of the river, though this feature is difficult to observe from the village. Access from the village street is through a lychgate. We dallied a few minutes to take some photographs and then pressed on with our walk.

As we left the village, the instructions and signs indicated that we should follow a lane leading to Blackford Farm. To the Thames Path walker keen to get back to the river again, this turned out to be quite a long and uninteresting country road. It was a good twenty-five minutes before we were out in the fields once more and the river appeared again close to the village of Kempsford. Kempsford church is visible across the fields, but it is not on the Thames Path. It had now turned out to be a warm sunny spring day. Pullovers needed for the chilly early morning were discarded and stowed away in rucksacks.

At Hannington Bridge we lost contact with the river again. The guidebook directed us along a road for a short distance and then onto an old bridle path to Inglesham. It was not an unpleasant route to follow, deep in the countryside and with only the birds for company. Since leaving Castle Eaton we had not encountered another human being. It was long past our normal lunchtime so we sat at the side of the path and ate our sandwiches and drank the last of the coffee from our flask. The sun had now reached full strength and as we sat there in its warmth it felt more like a summer's day than early April. A heron appeared quite close to us, a clear indication that the river was not far away, but it was completely out of sight, though the map showed it to be only a few fields distant. We resumed our walk, following the track with a hedge on one side and a ditch on the other for well over a mile, until we arrived at Upper Inglesham. The houses of this village are on either side of the A361. Here we were obliged to continue our walk along the busy road. It was not a pleasant diversion. The only provision for the walker is a grass verge, rather rough and uneven, though thankfully kept cut short. For a mile or so we plodded over this terrain, conscious of the cars that whizzed past us every few minutes. Eventually, in order to go in search of the Thames again, we had to cross the road to reach the lane leading to Inglesham church. Undertaking this maneouvre on a busy Saturday afternoon required some care. It was a relief to escape the traffic. We diverted for a few minutes to make the recommended visit to the church, which stands in an elevated position above the lane. This very old building is dedicated to St John the Baptist, and most information sources indicate that it was built in the 13th century, although some parts could be older than that. It is quite possible that it was built on the site of an earlier church. With its box pews and wall paintings, it gives the visitor the feeling of stepping into the past. It was a favourite church of William Morris, the writer and designer, and its restoration and preservation in Victorian times were largely due to him. Morris lived at Kelmscott Manor, which is close by, 2 miles on the other side of Lechlade. Sadly there is no local population to use the church: the houses of Inglesham village no longer exist. However, the church is still consecrated and is looked after by the Churches Conservation Trust.

After this brief interlude, we returned to the Thames Path sign and walked the way it pointed across a field. The river actually flows close to the church, but it is not possible to rejoin it there. It was of little importance, because the short walk across the field brought us to the Thames again. Sadly the encounter was of brief duration: on this last stretch into Lechlade a diversion was in operation. Fortunately we had the opportunity to observe and photograph one of the roundhouses. These were built as quarters for the lock-keepers of the Thames and Severn Canal, which used to connect with the Thames in the vicinity. The river Coln also joins the Thames at this point. The majority of trade traffic on the Thames and Severn Canal stopped around 1927 and it started to fall into decay. Now there are plans to restore at least some parts of it for use again.

Following the directions for the diversion led us away from the Thames and on a circular route into Lechlade. On the way we came across a well-trodden track with a sign that said 'Town Centre'. We decided to follow this and arrived in the main street at about three o'clock.

Lechlade, which was once called Letchlade, a pronunciation it still retains, is the highest point navigable on the Thames, though smaller boats can apparently continue a short distance beyond. The guidebook indicated that from here on there would be a towpath for our walk. Lechlade appears to be a smaller town than Cricklade, but it gained its important role as a staging post for goods and passengers during the heyday of the river and the adjoining canals. The town played a significant part in the wool trade and even Gloucestershire cheeses were shipped downstream from here. The 15th-century church of St Lawrence dominates the small market square. It was the market square that interested us: here, according to the bus information we had picked up, we would be able to catch a bus for Swindon. Spying a bus stop, we hurried over to it. The timetable confirmed that this was the stop for the nos. 64 and 74 to Swindon. We were in luck, because the next bus was due in a few minutes. Already a few people were assembling to catch it. The bus arrived on time and we settled back thankfully in our seats. The second section of our walk had been successfully completed. We both admitted that it had not been the best of walks. Quite large chunks of the route had been on tarmac roads and we hoped that there would not be too many diversions like this on the rest of the journey. However, once again we were well pleased with our efforts. We were not quite as tired as on the previous section and on the whole we had coped quite well with the different terrain we had walked. We felt that we were beginning to get into our stride as Thames Path walkers.

Once back in Swindon we made our way to the railway station and did not have long to wait for the next train to Reading. Once there, it would be an easy task to catch a bus for home and all we would have to do would be to sit back and enjoy the scenery. It was a pleasant ending to our third involvement with the Thames Path.

Lechlade To Newbridge

16.6 MILES (26.6 KILOMETRES)

It was not without some trepidation that we commenced the next section of the route. All the guidebooks described this part of the Thames Path as the remotest bit of the river. Except for a few pubs and farms there is little sign of habitation along the way. From our point of view it was also disconcerting to find out that there was no access to public transport at Newbridge – or close by, for that matter. In addition, in the back of our minds lurked the question of whether we would be able to complete the distance. At coming up to 17 miles, it would be the longest stretch of the route so far and indeed the longest walk we had ever contemplated. Careful planning was necessary if we were to have any chance of success.

At first, like many other Thames Path walkers we considered staying overnight somewhere. However, after investigating the travel arrangements, we decided that it should be possible to complete the leg in one day. The day before we were due to travel, I rang one of the taxi companies on the recommended list and spoke to Tony, who lived not far from Newbridge. He agreed to pick us up at Newbridge the following day and transport us back to Oxford after we had completed the walk. The only proviso was that this could not be later than 4.45 p.m. as he had another commitment after that. This put us under a bit of pressure, but we still considered we could make the deadline. The most critical aspect of the planning was that we needed to start out as early as possible. To do this meant catching a local train to London at the unearthly hour of 5.42 a.m.

In spite of our meticulous planning, the start to our day could have been better. I had experienced one of those 'bad' nights when sleep will not come. The situation was not helped by the early hour at which we needed to get up. As we set out I certainly did not feel prepared to walk 17 miles. On top of that, in spite of a reasonable weather forecast, we woke up to a cold grey day with a strong north-easterly wind blowing. Undeterred, we made our way to London and across to Paddington station for the train to Swindon. With a few minutes to spare before joining the train, we retreated to the Costa coffee store and indulged in our first coffee of the day. Costa Coffee. What a welcome refreshment stop this establishment proved to be! All along the route, in most sizeable towns we would find a Costa; and the bonus for us was that most would be open at eight in the morning, and very often earlier. To be able to sit down in comfort and have a hot drink before we started walking was one of the highlights of the trip. On top of that, in most of their shops it is possible to make a 'comfort stop'.

On arrival in Swindon we lost no time in walking the hundred yards to the bus station. With three visits behind us this was now a routine stroll, and we had ample time to catch the bus at a quarter to nine. Twenty-five minutes later it deposited us in the Market Square at Lechlade. We spent a little time looking around the little town, taking a few photographs and using the public conveniences (on the Thames Path one learns to take the opportunity) and then, conscious that we had a deadline to meet, we set out for the Ha'penny Bridge and our by now old friend the Thames. Ha'penny Bridge, which spans the river at this point, dates back to the 18th century and takes its name from the toll that was formerly charged for crossing it. The Toll House, a quaint square building, is still in place. We reached the riverbank via a path under the bridge, disturbing in the process a dozen or so mallards who were enjoying an after-breakfast nap, and then set off at a fairly brisk pace along the edge of the river. The Thames had now become quite a respectable width and the numerous moored boats were evidence of the traffic that had begun to use it. As we walked, the day was still grey and cool, with the north-easterly wind blowing in our faces. Few people were around other than an early-morning dog walker, who greeted us cheerfully.

A forty-minute walk brought us to St John's Lock, the first on the Thames, and nearby St John's Bridge, both named after the priory that once stood close by. At the edge of the lock stands a statue of Old Father Thames, gazing over the boats that pass through. He was originally commissioned for the Crystal Palace and was subsequently bought by the Thames Conservators and placed at the source of the Thames before being transferred to his present position in 1974. He probably has many more admirers where he is now. At this hour on a Saturday morning in April there was little activity at the lock, so with a nod in the direction of Old Father Thames, and the obligatory photograph, we were on our way again.

We were now in a fenced-off section that followed every curve of the river, with a clear indication of the route the walker must take. Not far away we could see Buscot church. Apparently there is an interesting parsonage there that dates back to the Queen Anne period and is now part of the National Trust's Buscot estate. For us a visit would have to wait until the future. It was at around this point that concrete pillboxes started to appear at intervals along the riverbank. These are a legacy from World War II and were built to defend the industrial Midlands. Stretching all along this section of the Thames, most are now abandoned, though we did see one taken over as a home for bats.

Buscot Lock was the next named landmark on our route; one of the smallest locks on the river, it was built in 1790, the same year as St John's Lock. After pausing for a few minutes to take in the scenery, we continued on our way.

Soon we passed close to the village of Kelmscott and Kelmscott Manor, both well hidden by trees. Kelmscott Manor was one of the homes of William Morris, who loved this part of the country and is buried in the churchyard of St George's, Kelmscott. With history a mere few yards away, it was tempting for us to linger for a visit to his former home. However, mindful of the distance we still had to cover, we dismissed the tentative idea and pressed on.

It was not long before we passed near the village of Eaton Hastings, just visible in the distance away to our right. The Thames at this stage twists and turns as it flows through the meadows. By this time the occasional pleasure craft would pass us and we would exchange a wave or greeting with the occupants. We were already beginning to experience the friendly atmosphere the river seems to generate. We came to Grafton Lock with its neat flower beds. Passing through a gate at the end, we continued to Radcot Bridge, the next landmark on our route.

We walked at a steady pace, conscious that there was still a long way to go, though this did not prevent us from enjoying the countryside. Frequently we would stop and take a photograph, Johanna more than I. She was always on the lookout for scenes or flowers that she could use in her hobby of making greetings cards. She was also keen to photograph some of the wildlife, mainly birds, but as is usually the case, most of them proved to be completely uncooperative when it came to having their picture taken.

The morning's weather remained grey, though it was warming up a little now. One minor distraction was that the wind seemed to blow directly in our faces for most of the time.

We could not help agreeing with the guidebooks about the remoteness of this section of the Thames. Since leaving the outskirts of Lechlade we had seen no one, apart from the few boats that came our way. We might have been many miles from anywhere, though in reality I guessed we were perhaps no more than 20 or so from Oxford.

It was ten to twelve when we reached Radcot Bridge, which carries one of the few roads in the area across the river. Claimed by many to be one of the oldest bridges on the Thames, it seems to have been built around 1200. The immediate habitation appeared to be a pub, aptly named the Swan Inn. We decided to allow ourselves a fifteen-minute break and half a pint of draught cider each. We had covered just over 6 miles of the journey and it had taken us a little over 2½ hours, making it an average around 2½ miles an hour. This was satisfying progress, but it would be necessary to maintain this pace to reach our destination on time. We were aware that we had not even reached the halfway mark. At the back of my mind was the thought that if we did discover that the effort and distance were too great, it might be possible to terminate our walk at Tadpole Bridge, 4 miles further on. No doubt the taxi would pick us up there just as easily as at Newbridge.

After our welcome rest, we resumed our walk. Once again the Thames twisted and turned through tranquil meadows and we followed the way it led, isolated, it seemed, from the rest of civilisation. The sun had now appeared from behind the clouds and was turning the afternoon into rather a pleasant one, though kept cool by the breeze that continued to blow. Not far from Radcot we came across Old Man's Bridge. From the river there is no indication of where those using this rather interesting wooden footbridge might come from or where it could help them get to. Nor did we find out who the old man was.

After another few miles we came to Rushey Lock, which some people consider to be one of the remotest on the river. There does not seem to be any definite information about how it got its name, but it could be from the rushes that grew here and were used to make mats and baskets. In order to reach the other side of the river, we had to walk across one of the lock gates. Fortunately, the one we wanted to use was closed at the time, so we were not delayed. The path crosses the lock-keeper's garden and then follows the access road to Tadpole Bridge. This was the first bit of tarmac we encountered on this section.

We kept up our steady pace along the quiet road, at one point just a bit worried that we might have gone wrong, and conscious that we did not have time to deal with any mistakes in navigation. All was well: a landmark loomed up, which could be none other than Tadpole Bridge. We wondered how it got this name; perhaps in the past it was a favourite hunting ground of young boys for tadpoles.

As we crossed the road, we noticed the solitary Trout Inn standing close to the 18th-century bridge. However, as we had already partaken of liquid refreshment at Radcot Bridge, we did not sample its hospitality. Rejoining the towpath was a satisfying feeling. At least 10 miles of the walk were now behind us. All thoughts of shortening our day's journey were dismissed. We pressed on. It was now just after one o'clock. Having had only an early breakfast supplemented by coffee and half a pint of cider, we were feeling decidedly peckish. Finding somewhere to stop and eat our packed lunch needed care to organise. We found ourselves walking through a forest of nettles. On and on it stretched, to either side of the path. The idea of sitting down for a lunch break here was definitely not inviting. We plodded on in silence, hoping that the growth of the irritating plant would come to an end. It did not. Eventually we spied another of the World War II pillboxes, right on the edge of the river. Its concrete base proved to be the perfect place to sit, free from nettles. We munched our sandwiches as we watched the water birds at work and play. It was incredibly peaceful just sitting there in the sun watching life on the water and listening to the breeze in the trees that line the river in this area. Even the plop, plop of a narrowboat making its way upstream seemed to fit in with the river life. The occupants, a middle-aged couple, gave us a friendly wave and greeting, to which we responded with equal enthusiasm.

Refuelled, we started on our way again. I was getting a bit concerned now that we seemed to have precious little time left if we were to reach Newbridge for the taxi. I think we both began instinctively to walk a bit faster. Now the Thames was flowing through an area of wetlands called Chimney Meadows Nature Reserve. This is claimed to be one of the largest areas of wild meadowland in England. Certainly the view from the bank of the Thames is of a huge area. It was quite pleasant with the spring sunshine beaming down on us, and we could hear curlews calling to each other. We stopped to chat to a young man who was walking in the opposite direction. When we asked him how far it was to Newbridge, he deliberated for a few seconds and then estimated that it would be about 5 miles. He thought we should make it with ease by a quarter to five. It was a comforting confirmation.

Tenfoot Bridge was the next landmark. This is a wooden footbridge that provides a link between Buckland and Chimney. The name has nothing to do with the size of the bridge but probably relates to the fact that there used to be a weir and a ten-foot-wide flash lock nearby. We walked on, following each twist and turn of the river. Occasionally a boat would pass us, but it was perhaps quite early in the season for a lot of river traffic. The map clearly indicated farms dotted here and there, including one away to our left called Chimney Farm, but from the river they were practically obscured from view.

Now we had to say goodbye to the Thames again. It wound its way off to the right in the direction of Duxford, and a new artificial section known as Shifford Lock Cut became our route. For the walker the change is hardly noticeable, except for the rather straight nature of the river. At one point we had to cross by bridge to the opposite bank. After the cut merged with the old river not far from Shifford weir we were out in the countryside again. In the distance we could just see a rather remote chapel and a few houses. The guidebooks state that these are the remnants of a much larger settlement. Legend has it that King Alfred the Great held a council of the English parliament there, so it would appear to have been a habitation of some standing in earlier times.

As the afternoon wore on, we became more confident of success. When we passed through the trees at the foot of Harrowdown Hill, we knew we were getting close to our goal. Leaving the trees behind, we were once again walking in pleasant meadowland, only this time it had all the appearance of being part of the farming community. Cows were grazing in the distance, though nearer the river the ground was taken up with colonies of swans and geese, who viewed us suspiciously.

Suddenly, in the distance we made out the unmistakeable signs of Newbridge: Newbridge Farm ahead of us to the right, the bridge itself straight ahead, and the two pubs, one at each end of the bridge. A glance at our watches showed us that we had almost an hour to spare, with no more than ten minutes' walking to go. A feeling of satisfaction started to creep in. We had done it. The steady pace we had kept up had now paid off in spite of all our doubts and concerns.

Tired but elated, we covered the last few steps. When we arrived at Newbridge, we discovered that although the bridge carries quite a busy road over the river, the only habitations are the two pubs, one of them called The Maybush and the other rejoicing in the name Rose Revived. Gratefully we sat down on one of the wooden seats outside The Maybush. Now all that was left was to ring Tony the taxi driver and see if he was free a bit earlier. What would we do without mobiles? Within thirty seconds I had reached him and he seemed quite pleased that we had telephoned early. He would be there in ten minutes. With such service, we could hardly grumble that we did not have time for a celebratory drink.

Tony arrived promptly, and quickly we were on our way to Oxford and the train home. In spite of our doubts we had done it: we had walked one of the longest stretches of the Thames Path we would be likely to encounter. We could not help but feel pleased with ourselves and with what we had accomplished. As we walked up the hill from the station to our house, the north-easterly wind that had been with us since the morning was still blowing mildly in our faces.

Newbridge To Oxford

14.1 MILES (22.6 KILOMETRES)

With one of the most challenging sections of the entire Thames Path walk behind us, and confident that we could meet the demands of longer walks, we looked forward eagerly to the next stage of our journey, from Newbridge to Oxford.

As it turned out this was to be scheduled for the bank holiday weekend at the beginning of May. Fine weather was forecast. Once again we made our now regular early start and 6.10 a.m. found us leaving our local railway station bound for Oxford, with just a quick change at Banbury to pick up the local train. As we travelled to Banbury, the early-morning mist was already clearing and the first signs of a pleasant sunny day were beginning to appear. At Banbury we were fortunate to catch an earlier train to Oxford and by half past seven we were experiencing a quiet early-morning atmosphere in the city.

To get to Newbridge, once again we were forced to enlist the help of a taxi. Tony was unavailable on this occasion, so I picked at random a taxi company on the list for Oxford and arranged for us to be picked up in the High Street at a quarter to nine. This gave us plenty of time for a pre-walk coffee in Caffè Nero and a chance to mull over the day ahead.

Just after half-past eight we emerged from our refreshment stop and headed to the pickup point agreed with the taxi company. Apprehensive that the taxi might not be there, I had made sure I had my mobile and the telephone number with me; but all was well: the taxi was waiting for us. Within two minutes we were on our way heading west and leaving Oxford behind. A minor hiccup occurred when the Croatian taxi driver did not know where Newbridge was, and I had not taken a note of the number of the road on which it was situated. However, perhaps more by good luck than good management, we arrived at Newbridge, on the A415, with the minimum of delay.

Waving goodbye to the friendly taxi driver, we lost no time in starting our walk. This time there was a pleasant feel to everything. For one thing we knew we were not putting ourselves under any sort of pressure to be in a certain place at a certain time. There was comfort in knowing that we were our own masters and that at the end of the walk there was a good train service home from Oxford. We had not even given any thought to the fact that even this walk would be more than 14 miles long.

It was around half past nine when we walked across the frontage of the Rose Revived to reach the towpath again. The sun was still hampered by clearing low cloud, so the grass was quite wet under our feet, but in spite of that walking conditions were quite enjoyable.

The Thames continued to wind its way through grassy fields. We passed another pillbox, standing stark and isolated, a further remnant of the 1939–45 war defences.

It did not seem to take us long to pass Hart's Weir Footbridge, which stands high on its legs, spanning the river in a gentle curve, inspiring its alternative name of Rainbow Bridge. At first sight it appears to be quite remote, surrounded only by fields, and we wondered why it was built. Apparently the answer is that once there was a weir here and the bridge was built in 1879 to serve local inhabitants. The weir was later dismantled, but the bridge remains as a right of way over the river. The weir had a number of other names during its history, including Ridge's, Rudges, and Butler's. A rather charming love story is connected with the area. One day in 1763, the young William Flower, Viscount Ashbrook, then an undergraduate at Oxford, came to the area close to the weir to fish. There he met and fell in love with the weir-keeper's daughter Betty Ridge (or Rudge). He was so determined to marry her that he paid for her to be sent away to receive an education and be groomed to be his wife. They married in nearby Northmoor Church in 1766 and appear to have had a happy marriage, producing heirs to the family line.

Soon after leaving Hart's Weir Bridge we came to Northmoor Lock, which was built in 1896, making it one of the later locks to be constructed on the Thames. It replaced Hart's Weir and is another reminder of the working days of the Thames.

We pressed on along the riverbank. In these early stages of the walk, the going is mostly on grass. The towpath as we always imagined it does not appear until much later on, except for short sections near habitation.

We approached Bablock Hythe just before eleven o'clock. Once an important crossing point on the river, now it has a rather holiday feel about it, with the modern Ferryman Inn being a focal point. We stopped for a few minutes to talk to an elderly couple who were staying at the nearby caravan site and enjoying a walk along the river. Bablock Hythe showed the important role the river now plays in providing a recreation outlet for boating enthusiasts. It was here that for the first time we came across numerous moored pleasure boats. The occupants chatted over a cup of tea while their children played ball on the grass nearby. At Bablock Hythe we again had to leave the river for a while and walk up the approach road. A comprehensive collection of chalets takes up the right-hand view of the road until after about five minutes the Thames Path sign appears again and points into a field on the right.

Here we had to make a decision. The guidebook suggests, if time permits, a visit to the nearby village of Stanton Harcourt. This would mean continuing up the road for about a mile or so. As we were not under any pressure to complete our walk by a certain time, we decided to give it a go. The hard road stretched ahead of us almost dead straight, a little bit uninteresting, with hedges on each side and the occasional tree. It is also a very quiet road: the only bit of activity we encountered was a woman on a bicycle. We were just beginning to wonder whether the detour was worth the extra effort, when the first houses of the village came into view.

The compact village proved to be well worth the detour. With its thatched cottages, manor house and church, it provided plenty of scope for our cameras. Stanton Harcourt has been much influenced by the Harcourt family, who can trace their ancestry back to Norman times and have owned the manor since that time. This no doubt accounts for the rather French look of the adjoining farmstead. The church of St Michael, which stands almost next door to the manor house, is also interesting and full of history. We pottered about the village for half an hour or so, at one stage divesting ourselves of pullovers and consigning them to our rucksacks, since the day had now become warm and sunny. Soon after that the Harcourt Arms beckoned and we decided to go inside for a drink. This proved to be a good choice. The atmosphere was warm and friendly and several of the locals were quite chatty. One man was very happy to talk about the village and its connection with the Harcourt family. He told us that the population of the village was about 500, though this figure according to the last census would be extremely low. When I explained that we were on the Thames Path walk, he politely reminded me that in this part of the country the Thames is known as the Isis. This is one of the oddities of the river. Above Oxford many people refer to it under this name, while some maps show it as 'Thames or Isis'. The strange thing is that it seems to be extremely difficult to obtain any information as to where the name originated.

Refreshed, we set off to rejoin the Thames Path. This meant retracing our steps along that long, uninteresting road, but this time –

perhaps due to the half-pint of cider we had consumed – it did not seem to take so long. By the time we reached the path, it came as no surprise to us that our interlude at Stanton Harcourt had used up nearly two hours, but we both agreed that it had been an excellent decision to go there.

Now the path led us into fields slightly away from the river, populated by flocks of sheep with their lambs, who looked at us inquisitively. It was now well past our lunchtime, so we sat on the grass at the edge of the field and munched our sandwiches, accompanied with coffee from the flask. It was very peaceful there.

Having resolved the pangs of hunger, we were on our way again. We took our time; it felt good just to be out here in the country surrounded by the sounds of nature. The warm afternoon sun shone down on us from a blue sky dotted with white puffy clouds. The instructions in the guidebook told us to head across one of the fields in the direction of the river. We carried out this manoeuvre, watched suspiciously by the sheep occupying the field as they munched the grass. We found the river without much effort; it flowed slowly between mudbanks. At this point we were a bit mystified. Though the guidebook was quite precise, the usual signs marking the position of the path were missing. We decided to follow the river and see what happened. This turned out to be a good strategy. We soon found a gate with the familiar yellow Thames Path sign on it.

Very soon we came to Pinkhill Lock, built in 1791. The name seems to be derived from a nearby farm. Here we had to cross the lock gates to reach the path on the other side of the river. As we left the lock behind, we met a young couple walking the Thames Path in the opposite direction and stopped and chatted for a few minutes. We told them about Stanton Harcourt and they seemed to think it would be a good idea to visit the village.

Not long afterwards we had to make a detour, as apparently the riverbank had been eroded. This meant a short walk to the road along a path between high fences. In the middle of this path we met a man striding out briskly. He stopped for a minute and explained that he was on his way to Tadpole Bridge as part of a sponsored walk. We asked him where he had started and he told us Abingdon. He also commented that his legs were getting tired. I did a quick mental calculation and came to the conclusion that he had already walked 15 miles or so and that there could be about the same again to his destination. It made our walk seem like an afternoon stroll! We wished him success on his mission and continued on our own trail. Two minutes' walk along the road, and a sign brought us back to the river beside a boatyard.

Once again the river meandered through fields, and we followed each turn on the edge of the bank. There were still a lot of sheep, but now they had been joined by a surprising number of geese, some with families, and these we passed carefully as they grazed under the watchful eye of the ganders. Each twist of the river unfolded a fresh view. There is a very peaceful atmosphere on this section. Though the nearest sizeable town is probably no more than a few miles away at any point, this is not apparent to the walker. From time to time pleasure boats would pass us, but their gentle pace seemed to fit in with the mood of the river, and their sound was not intrusive. As they passed us their crews would wave or acknowledge our greeting. The river seems to bring out sociability in everybody.

We reached Swinford Bridge, one of the last two toll bridges left on the river. Apparently, by tradition, the owner pays no tax on the toll revenue. This magnificent stone bridge was built in the 18th century by the Earl of Abingdon to carry travellers journeying from London to Cheltenham over the river. At one time the road crossing here was the main A40, but when a bypass was built round nearby Eynsham the road had to accept the lower status B4044. Pedestrians cross the road free, but our route led us beneath one of the graceful arches. We read that the name is derived from 'swine ford' (a crossing on the river for pigs), which seems quite logical.

Only a short distance from Swinford Bridge is Eynsham Lock, built in 1928 and thus one of the newest on the river. We felt it justified some photographs, so we spent a few minutes snapping a cruiser using the lock.

Shortly after this the landscape changed and we found a large plantation on our right. This is Wytham Great Wood, a 600-acre expanse of woodland owned by Oxford University and used for conservation research. The information sheet told us that it is a great habitat for birds and wildlife. This was the first time on our walk that we had been close to woodland.

The next point of interest was King's Lock. On the placid waters approaching the lock a solitary rower in a boat waited patiently for the gates to open. For the rest of the journey we came across him a few times. Sometimes he would gain on us and at other time we would overtake him. We lost him eventually on the approach to Oxford. We discovered that King's Lock was one of the most interesting so far on our journey. It was built in 1928, but there are records of a weir here dating back to the 13th century. The lock is fascinating because the northern part of it appears to be on an island that almost conceals the start of the stretch of waterway known as Duke's Cut, which connects the Thames with the Oxford Canal. Another feature of the lock is only apparent on close inspection. The newly erected visitor centre is built entirely from low-carbon or locally sourced materials. The foundations are made from used car tyres, and the walls are constructed from straw bales with lime plaster. The electricity comes from photovoltaic cells on the roof. We read that if this building proves to be a success, it is hoped to use the same process for other building along the Thames.

We stopped to take some photographs and then, conscious that we still had quite a way to go before we reached Oxford, we pressed on. After about half an hour it became clear that our goal was not so distant now. The bridge that carries the A34 over both the river and our path loomed up – a landmark that was now familiar to us. We walked underneath as cars and lorries whizzed across above our heads. Very soon afterwards we came to the ruins of Godstow Abbey, nestling in its meadows. The abbey was founded in 1139, and it was in this area that King Henry II met his mistress Rosamund Clifford, known as Rosamund the Fair. When she died she was buried in the abbey. The remaining stone walls with their glassless windows reach up to the sky, giving just an inkling of the majestic building that once stood here.

Godstow Lock, which dates back to 1790, is nearby. Also close at hand is the well-known and picturesque Trout Inn, a building that was once part of the abbey.

This section of the river is claimed to be the place where Lewis Carroll first found inspiration for *Alice in Wonderland.*

Now that we were close to Oxford, a surprising number of people were about, clearly residents of Oxford and the surrounding area out for an afternoon walk or enjoying a gentle little stroll in the warm mid-afternoon sunshine. The river is quite wide at this point, and on the opposite bank we could see the expanse of Port Meadow, which has been common land for centuries. It stretches away from the river, providing grazing for cows and sheep. Some were venturing into the shallows of the river, completely oblivious to the nearby boats.

A sign pointed away from the river indicating refreshments available in the Perch Inn at Binsey. Though this was tempting, we did not allow it to distract us, intent as we were on reaching our destination. We had now been walking for almost eight hours with no more than an hour's break in total. All our concentration was on reaching Oxford, which still seemed to be several miles off.

At Bossom's Boatyard we had to cross to the other bank of the river by way of the rather pretty Medley Footbridge. Now the towpath proper traversed a leafy route alongside moored boats. Quite a few people passed us, and the number of bicycles on the path increased. We guessed that the centre of Oxford was not far away. This was welcome knowledge as we were both feeling tired. For once the sound of a steam train puffing away on the railway track somewhere over to our left did not prompt me to investigate. We crossed the feeder entrance to the Oxford Canal and passed the backs of some cottages, and suddenly Osney Bridge was in front of us. We had made it.

It was only a few minutes' walk from Osney Bridge to the railway station. Rather weary but again elated, we walked the last few yards. It was exactly half past five when we reached the station and a welcome sit-down on a platform seat to wait for our train. The walk had been long but full of variety. We had covered an extremely pleasant section of the river, and had negotiated the more remote parts of the path. The next sections after Oxford would eventually lead us to the Thames Valley, where the river winds its way through the Cotswolds on its way to the sea. We knew that this area would be different from the sections we had already walked, but we looked forward with enthusiasm to exploring these parts of the Thames Path.

Oxford To Abingdon

9.8 MILES (15.7 KILOMETRES)

On the next section of the route we decided to deviate from the guidebook. Instead of walking from Oxford to Culham as suggested, we opted to walk from Oxford to Abingdon, which is 2 miles shorter. The logical reason for this was the ease of transport from both towns. It appeared that getting back home from Culham would involve several changes on the bus journey, whereas Abingdon has an excellent bus service to Oxford. Why the guidebook indicates Culham as the start and finish of a walk is possibly the rail connection, while we were relying on buses.

Yet again we had to make an early start, and soon after six o'clock we were on the train for Banbury, where we were again lucky to catch the earlier train to Oxford, this time with less than a minute to spare. When we arrived in Oxford, we decided to walk the first mile of the path, from Osney to Folly Bridge, before stopping for our customary early-morning coffee.

Retracing our final steps of the previous walk, we returned to Osney Bridge. We had followed this section of the route through Oxford on previous visits, so it was familiar territory. It is a pleasant walk that follows the river as it winds its way through the city. For most of the way the banks of the river are lined with buildings, and we passed a few warehouses and boatyards, yet surprisingly there is quite a bit of greenery in places. At one point trains rumble overhead on the main railway line to Oxford.

From Osney Bridge, steps lead down to the riverbank. Here the river is separated by a narrow patch of green and a service road from a row of terraced houses that stretches for a hundred yards or so with a view over the river. Narrowboats are moored peacefully next to the towpath. Everything was quiet and tranquil so early in the morning. The sky overhead was still grey, but with a hint of better things to come.

We walked along, taking the occasional photograph, with only the water birds for company. The Waterman's Arms came into view, a legacy from the days of the working Thames. Many a boatman would have partaken of a glass of ale there to lighten the day. Now the pub is a convenient stop for pleasure boats, or even Thames Path walkers who want to quench their thirst. Shortly after the Waterman's Arms, Osney Lock appears and the path diverts round it for a few yards. When we passed there was no activity at the lock and the water birds had it to themselves. The path wanders past Grandpont Nature Reserve, which was created on the site of the old gasworks: 7 acres (3 hectares) of nature, only a short distance from the city centre.

After about twenty-five minutes the towpath led us past more residential buildings and then suddenly we were at Folly Bridge. There has been a bridge carrying the Abingdon road across the river here for centuries, but the guidebooks tell us that this stone one was built in 1825–7. Apparently it has been called other names in its history, including Grand Pont and South Bridge. The current name is said to derive from the folly that once stood nearby. The original house was demolished many years ago, but a replacement stands there today, an unusual building with various statues attached to it. According to one guidebook we read, the 13th-century philosopher Roger Bacon lived for a while in a house close to the bridge. Climbing up onto the bridge, we decided it was worth a photograph and spent five minutes on the other side of the road waiting for gaps in the early morning traffic so that we could get a reasonable picture.

At Folly Bridge we left the river and walked the short distance into Oxford town centre to have a coffee break. This time we abandoned our regular Costa or Nero stop: our destination was the café vault of St Mary's Church, close to the High Street, an old haunt of ours. Unfortunately, on this occasion, even though we arrived there well past the opening time of half past eight, the staff were not quite ready for business, so there was some delay before we could have our long-anticipated coffee and cake. After this short break and with renewed vigour we set forth again to Folly Bridge.

It was almost half past nine by the time we were back at the river. On a Saturday morning in spring the towpath in Oxford is a busy place. We made our way past walkers, joggers and cyclists, while enthusiastic coaches on bicycles shouted instructions to the rowing teams practising on the water. Every few minutes it seemed we were stepping aside to avoid a collision. We were only able to identify one of the rowing teams, who had the word 'Exeter' printed on their tracksuits. Across the river the tree-lined banks of Christ Church Meadows provided a backdrop to our view. Except for the crowded towpath it was pleasant walking alongside the river on this bright May morning.

When you leave Oxford by way of the river, it is surprising how quickly the buildings disappear into the distance. In no time at all the walker has the beauty of the river on one side of the towpath and meadows on the other. What is quite noticeable is the increasing width of the river and the mounting number of craft. Gone was the dreamy, lonely Thames of the earlier walks: now we were walking beside a busy waterway that carried four or five times as much traffic. It seemed hardly any time at all before Iffley Meadows, a huge expanse of ancient wetlands totalling 90 acres (36 hectares), appeared on our left. Both here and in other marshy areas adjoining the Thames, the keen botanist with sharp eyes can discover the snake's-head fritillary growing wild.

These beautiful plants flower in April or May, and Johanna had managed to photograph some on the previous section of our walk. On this occasion we did not see any, though a more intensive search might have led to a sighting of this rarity.

On this section of the walk we felt quite relaxed due to the short distance involved. Our rearranging of the route had brought it down to just over 10 miles, a mere hop compared to some of the previous sections. Our easy pace soon brought us to Iffley Lock, one of the oldest locks on the river. Beyond the lock the towpath traffic lessened considerably, the peace of the river disturbed only by the occasional walker, the water birds and the odd pleasure craft passing us. This part of the river is remarkably lush, with meadows on one side and a high bank of trees and vegetation on the other.

The picturesque Sandford Lock, with the King's Arms alongside, is the next landmark along this stretch. The name gives a clue to its possible origin: 'a sandy ford'. All along the path of the river Thames there have been crossing points for centuries, many in place before records started; Oxford, 'a crossing used by oxen', is another. According to the records, the first purpose-built lock at Sandford dates to around 1631–2. However, this is not the one we see today, because it has been rebuilt. For many years there was also a mill here. When we arrived, several people were enjoying the scene and we stopped to chat to a charming elderly lady out for a trip on her bicycle, complete with pet poodle in the front basket. She told us that she had moved to the area from Rutland and that in her spare time she made little purses, which she sold to support the Battersea Dogs' and Cats' Home – an establishment we were to pass much later on our Thames Path walk.

Locks are interesting places; there is always the temptation to linger a while and just watch the world go by, or, to be more precise, observe the calm, leisurely activity. Perhaps that is why there always appear to be a few seats around for people who want to stop and stare. They are excellent places for photographs and we both took advantage of the opportunity. At one point I became so engrossed in my photographic efforts that I suddenly 'lost' Johanna. She had found something rather interesting. I came upon her busy trying to take a photograph of an almost hidden stone bearing a plaque that read: 'A ferry existed at Sandford as early as the 13th century and this mounting stone was used by riders to remount after crossing the river.'

Sadly this picturesque spot is tinged with tragedy. The waters of the weir, known as the Sandford Lasher, are dangerous and there is a monument to five Oxford students who drowned there. One of these was Michael Llewelyn-Davies, foster son of J. M. Barrie, the creator of *Peter Pan*.

After Sandford Lock comes an even more lush wild stretch of river. We passed the road to Radley and of course Radley station – a blessing for those who want to break off the walk at this point. But we pressed on, arriving eventually at the boathouse used by Radley College, a nearby public school with a keen tradition of rowing. Not far on we caught sight of Nuneham House, another lesser-known minor stately home, just visible nestling in trees a little distance away on the other side of the river. The original house was built in the 18th century by Earl Harcourt, one of King George III's courtiers, but it has been altered several times during its history. It is recorded that the Earl had a whole village demolished and removed to another location to allow Capability Brown more scope to design and landscape the surroundings. From 1942 to 1957 the house was used by the RAF, and it is now owned by Oxford University. An intriguing feature on the nearby hill almost overlooking the house is a piece of local history known as the Carfax Conduit, an ornate tower-like structure originally built in the centre of Oxford to carry a system of lead pipes used to supply clean water to the city. In the 18th century, when the road where it stood was widened, it was acquired by Earl Harcourt, who moved it to its present location.

It now became apparent that Abingdon, our goal, was getting closer. We spied the spire of the 12th-century St Helen's church on the horizon. Foot traffic became more frequent, with many people out for the day, including one couple we met who were walking the Green Belt Way around Oxford. We were now amongst trees and scrubland, pleasant and remote, though the trappings of civilisation were never far away. At one point the towpath passes under a railway bridge with long-distance trains thundering overhead. Oddly, the sound does not seem to disturb the flocks of water birds that congregate on the river around this area. The Thames appears to be host to an amazing number of Canada geese, who seem to spend most of their time paddling in the river and resting on the riverbank, interspersed with the occasional formation flight.

On the approach to Abingdon there is a rather interesting section of the river known as Swift Ditch (marked 'Back Water' on some maps), which leaves the main river on the opposite bank and bypasses Abingdon completely, in the process creating Andersey Island. Some sources suggest that it is the original path of the river; others appear to think that it may have been an artificial channel. It is no longer navigable. It meets up with the main river again just before Culham, which would be further along our Thames Path walk.

We had one last detour before we reached the outskirts of Abingdon. This was a rather muddy path that winds its way through thickets a short distance from the Thames. Quite close by here is another artificial waterway, the Abbey Stream, believed to have been cut by the Abingdon monks many years ago to provide access to the river and supply water to the nearby mill.

As we made our way along the tree-lined path, we met a young couple with their little son; we chatted for a few minutes and learned that they were also walking the Thames Path. Like so many others we had encountered, however, they were travelling from the Thames Barrier to the source. We began to wonder if we were the only ones walking downhill to the sea.

The diversion ended at Abingdon Lock and weir and reunited us with the main river. A leisurely stroll over the lock bridge brought us into parkland beside the Thames, providing a pleasant entrance to Abingdon.

It was half-past one when we arrived at Abingdon Bridge, a fine 15th-century stone-arched structure, which spans the Thames at the edge of the town and carries the A415. We climbed up onto the road, which leads into the town, and visited the nearby Nag's Head riverside pub for a welcome glass of cider. Half an hour later we sat in the sunshine overlooking the river activity and ate our long-overdue lunch. After that we made a brief exploration of the town itself.

Once the county town of Berkshire, Abingdon became part of Oxfordshire in 1974, when counties were rearranged, some of them disappearing forever. It is a very old town that has seen many changes. Roman remains have been found and it appears to have been well established by Saxon times. Abingdon Abbey was founded in 675 and became a very important religious establishment. In modern times the town was once the home of MG cars, but that era passed, like the town's association with the railway, which ended for passengers in 1963. A supermarket stands on the site of the railway station, and now passengers have to travel to Radley or Didcot to catch a train.

Our first impressions revealed a compact little town with quite a pleasant atmosphere. The County Hall has a prominent position in the small central square and there is still an old-world feel to the surrounding area. Fortunately, the new shopping area close by tends to be discreet. We wandered into the Visitor Information Office and the woman behind the counter told us where we could catch a bus for Oxford. It was a good thing we enquired, because the bus stop appeared to be on a kind of ring road encircling the town centre. It took us a few minutes to walk there and after a short wait we caught the bus back to Oxford, courtesy of the Oxford Bus Company and our bus passes.

We had completed section five of the Thames Path and now we felt well equipped to deal with any of the walking involved. We looked forward to each new section with enthusiasm.

Abingdon To Wallingford

13.5 MILES (21.6 KILOMETRES)

The morning held the promise of another warm May day as again we caught the early train to Banbury. Once there, we had another quick dash over the footbridge to catch the local train to Oxford, which was waiting on the other platform. Twenty minutes later we arrived in Oxford to find the X3 bus for Abingdon waiting outside the station. It was just after half-past seven, and there were few passengers on the bus, but we chatted to a middle-aged couple who were walking the Green Belt Way and, like us, were using public transport to get them to parts of the route.

As soon as we arrived in Abingdon, which was already basking in the sunshine, we savoured our usual pre-walk coffee in the Costa store conveniently situated across the road from the bus stop and already open for business. Half an hour later we made the five-minute walk down the street to Abingdon Bridge, where the day's section of our walk along the river would commence. As we had diverted from Oxford to Abingdon the previous week, this time we had to add a few miles to the journey outlined in the guidebook. This brought the total to 13½ miles, but after some of our previous marathons this did not concern us unduly, and once again we set out with the knowledge that there was no pressure on us to be at a certain point by a certain time.

From Abingdon the walk is along the north bank of the Thames, and soon becomes bordered by open fields and meadows. Across the river we could see a line of neat houses with well-tended gardens that extended down to the riverbank. It was pleasant walking, the grass wet with dew drying quickly in the strengthening rays of the morning sun.

It seemed quite a short walk to Culham. On the way we passed the spot where the abandoned Swift Ditch, which we had seen on the previous walk, rejoins the main river. The village of Culham is fairly close by, but we decided not to detour and explore it, an opportunity we regretted later because apparently it is quite picturesque, with its old manor house, church and cottages. The records tell us that Culham was once a much bigger village, but the reason for the decline in its population is obscure; it has been suggested that this may have been due to the Black Death or poor harvests. We passed nearby Culham Lock, peaceful and unoccupied so early on a Saturday morning, and then it was on again through the greenery surrounding the river.

By now the river had become a fairly reasonable size. Here and there were the remnants of its working life, with new sections cut to eliminate the numerous bends and speed up commercial traffic. Today that part of the river's life has long since gone and pleasure craft have taken over, either slick cabin cruisers or narrowboats. As the morning wore on, both kinds passed us from time to time and we usually exchanged a friendly wave with the occupants.

The village of Appleford came into view, away in the distance on the opposite bank. The church spire is a rather unusual fat shape and can be seen for quite a distance. Also visible were the cooling towers of Didcot power station, which appear on the horizon shortly after Abingdon and remain in view until way after Dorchester.

Clifton Cut, another channel dug to bypass the bends in the river, announced to us the nearness of Clifton Hampden village and, very soon afterwards, Clifton Hampden Lock. Compared to some of the other locks on the river, Clifton is quite a youngster: it was built in

1822. We now had our first sight of Clifton Hampden Bridge, gracefully spanning the river ahead of us. A picturesque red brick structure with elegant arches, it was designed by Sir George Gilbert Scott and opened in the 1860s. With the church in the background, it is a scene that must have been photographed many times, and we also stopped to capture the view on our cameras.

The river passes close by the village, and guidebooks recommend a visit. As the detour required only a short walk, we happily followed this advice. It proved to be well worthwhile: Clifton Hampden with its thatched cottages, pubs and post office is indeed a pretty village, a reminder of times past, and we could not help wondering what it must have been like perhaps two centuries ago when it relied on agriculture and the river for its sustenance. The church of St Michael and All Angels is interesting, because it stands on a high mount overlooking the river. To reach it we had to climb a short flight of steps from the road. Apparently a church has stood here for a long time, parts of the present structure dating back to at least the 13th century. Jerome K. Jerome, in his delightful book *Three Men in a Boat,* mentions Clifton – and the Barley Mow pub, which is not very far away.

After we had explored the village to our satisfaction, we made our way back to the bridge to cross to the opposite bank and rejoin the path. The panorama of green fields continued as we followed the river towards the next major landmark, Day's Lock. Shortly after we passed the village of Burcot, almost completely hidden from view on the opposite bank, we were both quite surprised when the lock suddenly appeared. This was the halfway point of our day's walk and we felt quite pleased with ourselves to have reached it so quickly.

Day's Lock was quite busy when we arrived. It was built in 1789 and is apparently named after a local family. From there we had a good view of the small wooded hills known as Wittenham Clumps, notable for the fine viewpoint they offer those willing to climb to the top. At the lock it was necessary to change over to the other side of the river again.

Soon the well-known village of Dorchester loomed up on the horizon, and a path pointed to it temptingly. At first we ruled out a visit, thinking that time was against us and that it would have to be a pleasure for another day. However, a short distance further on, another path to Dorchester appeared. This time the village was definitely nearer, and we changed our minds. This turned out to be a good decision. Dorchester is a pretty village full of history reaching back to Roman times. Once a great abbey stood here, on or close to the site of a Saxon cathedral dedicated to St Birinus, but all that remains is the medieval church of St Peter and St Paul, which dates back to the 12th century, and a few other buildings. The guidebook tells us that after the dissolution of the monasteries a rich merchant bought the church and gave it to the people of the parish. In bygone times Dorchester was an important coaching stop. In the 18th century there were as many as ten inns, of which several remain, providing a safe and welcome refuge for passengers travelling between London and Oxford. There is more than enough of interest in the village to occupy an afternoon, and numerous establishments in which to partake of refreshment when the visitor is weary of sightseeing. We certainly intend to go there again when we have more time to spend. Our brief sojourn on this occasion was halted when we retreated to the 16th-century Fleur de Lys Inn and enjoyed half a pint of excellent cool draught cider.

It was almost an hour before we made our way back to the Thames and continued on our way. Shillingford was the next listed landmark. Just before the village it is necessary to leave the towpath and cross a field to the rather busy road that passes through Shillingford. Fortunately there is an adequate footpath and it is only five minutes' walk into the village, where the turnoff point back to the river is clearly marked. The road leads to a network of footpaths that lead between high walls at one point. We passed the gates of Shillingford Court and then circled around it as we returned to the river. On this section there are some rather interesting markers, which show the highest flood levels over the years.

We joined the towpath again on a pleasant leafy section close to Shillingford Bridge. A handful of pleasure cruisers were moored close by and there was pedestrian activity on the towpath. Several people were in fact on the Thames Path trail, though once again walking the opposite way to us. We pondered yet again the reason for choosing to do so. For us the excitement of the plan was to trace the great river from its humble beginnings in a Gloucestershire field to its meeting with the sea in London. The attraction of watching the river grow in size and the changes it goes through as it winds its way were paramount. However, it is possible that folk walking in the other direction find pleasure in watching it grow smaller and more remote. Place of residence seems to play a major part in which route to choose. We found that many of the people we met who lived at a considerable distance from the river had chosen to walk from source to barrier. It would be interesting to know the percentage of each group.

Back on the river, we enjoyed the afternoon sunshine. It is only a gentle stroll from Shillingford to the next point of interest, the small Thames-side village of Benson, known as Bensington before its name changed in the 19th century. It was well established in Saxon times and is recorded in the Domesday Book. Like Dorchester it was a staging post for coaches between London and Oxford. It was a key battle site during the civil war and is alleged to have been one of the last Royalist strongholds overcome by Cromwell's forces. As it is situated in a frost hollow, it is notable for sometimes recording the lowest temperatures in the UK. The area is perhaps more widely known for the nearby airbase at RAF Benson, which was built just before World War II and played a major part in that conflict.

Without diverting from the route, the Thames walker does not get an opportunity to see much of the village. The towpath ends in a mass of hire cruisers and a large tea room. For the first time on our journey we encountered quite a lot of people in one place at one time. The fine afternoon seemed to have brought out many of the local population, who were enjoying the recreation of the riverside, mingling with the crews of the various leisure boats tied up nearby. We walked past the tea room and made for the adjoining grassed area just beyond, which was not too crowded. Sitting on a convenient bench, we finished the coffee in our thermos flask, taking a well-earned rest at the same time.

As we set off again we had to make another short detour away from the river. Along the Thames Path these diversions crop up from time to time. Sometimes this is due to bank erosion or some form of repair taking place, but at other times the reason is more obscure, particularly when the way ahead is blocked by what looks like modern building. We wondered how this would have come about, and why the towpath had not been left as a right of way. No doubt there is a logical and simple explanation for building so close to the river.

On this occasion the diversion was of short duration: a few minutes' walk down the nearby road, and once again we turned back towards the river and Benson Lock. The current lock was built in 1788, but apparently there are records of a mill and weir here in the 14th century. This lock has the honour of being one of the two locks on the Thames that are the greatest distance apart. It shares this distinction with Cleeve Lock, 6½ miles (10.4 km) downstream. At Benson Lock we had to cross the river. Formerly there was a ferry here, but now there is a long footbridge, which proved to be a very good location for some work with our cameras. Once on the other side of the river, we found ourselves on a riverside path heading straight for Wallingford, our day's destination. It was an easy walk, with the river on one side and more or less open meadowland on the other. By now we were meeting a few people, most of whom seemed to be residents of Wallingford out for an afternoon stroll, though at one point we were overtaken by a young man who had all the appearance of being a dedicated walker, except for one thing: instead of boots or shoes, he strode out firmly in flip-flops. With a courteous 'Thank you', he overtook us and disappeared into the distance.

Soon the spire of Wallingford's St Peter's church made a welcome appearance. Our goal was in sight. On the approach to the town the ruins of Wallingford Castle, dating back to Norman times, loomed up on our right. Wallingford stood for the king during the civil war, and when the Royalists lost their cause, Oliver Cromwell gave orders that the castle was to be destroyed. Like nearby Benson, it lays claim to being one of the last Royalist fortresses to succumb to Cromwell's army.

After this encounter with history, it was not long before we arrived in Wallingford itself. Our walk ended close to the fine twenty-two-arch bridge that spans the river there. It was only a short distance along the High Street to the Market Square, from where, we had been told, the buses for Oxford departed. Just to make sure, we stopped a passer-by and checked. She confirmed that the bus left from in front of the town hall. A few minutes later we arrived at the tiny Market Square. The square is dominated by the elegant town hall, which dates back to 1670. Wallingford was once an important town, even in Saxon times. There was a mint here at one period of its history. While searching for the bus stop we noted that the tourist information centre was housed in the town hall, though it was closed by the time we arrived. Seeing a bus stop, we assumed that this was where we needed to wait. We were just checking the details on the timetable when I spied a bus turn and park in front of the town hall, a few steps away. Conscious that the buses to Oxford were not very frequent, we hurried over to it. We need not have worried, as it waited there for several minutes. Soon we were on our way, thankful to sit back in the comfortable seat and watch the scenery pass by. We had completed another leg of the Thames Path. We were beginning to realise that each section was different from the previous one. Perhaps it is the varying scenery that makes this walk attractive to so many people. We looked forward to what the next section might bring.

SECTION SEVEN

Wallingford To Reading

18.5 MILES (29.6 KILOMETRES)

After walking the Abingdon to Wallingford section of our route in pleasant sunshine, it was disappointing that on the next few Saturdays the weather was decidedly inclement. While neither of us objected to walking in the rain, we both felt that to enjoy the route to its full, it was better to wait for the right day to turn up than set out to walk in bad weather conditions just for the sake of saying we had done so. In addition, taking photographs is to be preferred when the weather is fine. We had had experience of being out and about in rain trying to take photographs while keeping the camera dry, and we did not relish the thought of having to do that again.

As June 13th loomed up, we scanned the weather forecast anxiously, hoping that this Saturday there would be a change in the weather for the better. On the Friday, the BBC forecast white cloud and a warm temperature for the next day. With this promise, we decided to go.

It meant yet another early start. We had checked the travel arrangements and discovered that we could reach Wallingford by bus, changing at Reading. The first bus to Reading left our local bus station at 6.50 a.m., and just before departure time we arrived at the bus bay to find our transport already sitting there and the driver busy reading his newspaper. I think he was surprised to see two pensioners with bus passes so early in the day. A few minutes later the motor rumbled into life and we were on our way, with a rather leaden sky overhead.

It took about an hour to reach Reading. We had over half an hour to wait for the bus that would take us on to Wallingford, so after checking where the bus stop was we retreated to the nearby railway station in search of a comfort stop and some refreshment. Reading station has been rebuilt and is well laid out, with good services. It also has a Costa, which we found convenient. The surroundings were not quite as comfortable as in a high-street Costa store, but the coffee was well up to the usual standard.

A few minutes before the X40 bus was due we made our way to the bus stop. The gloomy sky was beginning to fade away, revealing glimpses of sunshine, and by the time we reached Wallingford half an hour later the morning had turned into a sunny one. It looked like a good omen for the rest of the day. We did not waste too long retracing our steps to where the previous walk had ended, but just spent a few minutes on the way taking a few photographs. The guidebook instructed us to turn off at the bottom of the High Street into the aptly named Thames Street. This led us to St Leonard's church, and after we had skirted round the churchyard, a few minutes' walk brought us back to our old friend the Thames, quiet and peaceful in the early morning.

We set off at a steady pace along the towpath, conscious that we had a long walk ahead of us if we were to reach Reading that day. Because we had revised our itinerary, the walk would amount to around 18 miles. This would be even longer than the Lechlade to Newbridge section, but we were less concerned because the stretch ahead of us was not in a remote area. The walk ahead of us today would be through well-populated countryside, with bus and rail links nearly everywhere. We had set out with the comfort of knowing that if we grew tired later in the day and found the distance a bit too much for us, there was always the possibility of breaking short the walk and catching public transport back to Reading.

After leaving Wallingford, it was not long before we were walking through pleasant meadows beside the river. The water flowed quiet and undisturbed on our left; at this hour on a Saturday morning most of the occupants of the pleasure boats were probably having a late breakfast, so the wildlife had the river to themselves. Mallards were in abundance, along with moorhens and coots, while occasionally we would spot a heron resting on a convenient perch. Very soon we passed the sign that directs the walker to Cholsey and its railway station. This is the station at which the guidebook finishes the previous leg of the Thames Path.

The weather forecast proved to be accurate, for it was a pleasant sunny morning with hardly a breeze blowing: ideal walking conditions. We were now making our way along the edge of the Cholsey Marsh nature reserve, and the peace and tranquillity of the river and the adjoining natural habitat were really something to experience. It felt almost a privilege to be able to be part of the scene and walk listening to the sounds of nature. Eventually the towpath led us to a railway viaduct spanning the river, which we walked under to the accompaniment of a train passing overhead. The serenity of the morning was broken as the trappings of civilisation made an appearance.

Not long after this the guidebook indicated that it was necessary to leave the river for a short distance and walk through the nearby village of Moulsford, which sits on a busy road. A track leads to the interestingly named Offlands Farm, and a left turn here brought us to the A329. We walked along the welcome pavement, passing the church of St John the Baptist as we looked for our turn-off, Ferry Lane, which eventually appeared on our left when we had almost reached what looked like the end of the village. From here a short walk brought us back to the river at the Beetle and Wedge Boathouse inn and restaurant. The odd name is derived from the mallet and wedge used to split timber and appears to be associated with wooden clog-making. We had to walk down beside the inn to reach the river. Suddenly we found ourselves in the midst of a golden wedding celebration that was taking place on the area in front of the inn facing the river. We politely made our way through to the Thames Path.

Soon we were out in the countryside again, walking through meadows along the edge of the river. At one point we could see South Stoke church across the water. Cleeve Lock came into sight, which indicated to us that we had covered a distance of 5 or 6 miles since leaving Wallingford. It also told us that we were getting close to Streatley and Goring. First built in 1787, Cleeve Lock has the smallest fall of all the locks on the river, at just 2ft 3in (0.69 m). It also has the shortest distance from the next lock, only half a mile separating it from Goring Lock. It was nearly midday, and the river was now becoming busier. Quite a few boats had passed us on the way from Moulsford and as a result Cleeve Lock was now in steady use.

Beyond the lock a short section brought us within sight of Goring Lock and its neighbour Streatley. It also meant another brief diversion. We followed a path that led us around the side of Streatley church and ended on the road leading to the bridge that spans the river to link the two villages of Streatley and Goring. Until 1837 there was only a ferry here, but today the bridge is busy with traffic. It also connects two counties: Goring is in Oxfordshire, while Streatley is in Berkshire. Both villages are well known to walkers. Several major walks, including the Thames Path and the Ridgeway, meet at the river here. The guidebook informed us that we were now in the area known as Goring Gap, the valley the Thames cut for itself when it decided to change its direction of flow at the end of the last ice age.

The path joined the road close to the entrance of the Swan Hotel, a popular riverside hostelry. Finding ourselves outside an establishment that was likely to offer liquid refreshment, we ventured in. It turned out to be rather upmarket, with waiter service for the drink we required. We sank gratefully into leather chairs and ordered two ciders. For the second time that day we found ourselves in the midst of a celebration. A wedding reception was being held and quite a lot of the guests from 'over the border' were dressed in kilts. Not until we were actually inside the building did we realise that the hotel had river frontage, and that quite a crowd of people were having lunch sitting on the terrace overlooking the river. We sipped our cider, watching the events going on around us and then, ever conscious that several miles still lay ahead of us, we decided to resume our day's walk. After a minor delay in finding somebody who would take our payment for the cider, we were on our way, somewhat subdued by the price of the drink, which we thought was a bit on the high side.

Our route now took us across the bridge, and almost immediately we were back on the towpath. Hardly had we rejoined it when we found an excellent piece of green on which to have our lunch. We stopped to chat with another couple who were also walking the Thames Path. On this particular section we met several other walkers intent on completing the distance, but yet again all were walking in the opposite direction to us.

With our late lunch behind us, we set off again along the towpath, taking in the scenery and watching the increased activity on the river. It was well populated with pleasure boats, slowly moving up- or downstream. They were now passing further away from us, due to the increased width of the river, so the cheery greeting of earlier sections began to diminish. For a while we walked through pleasant meadows as the Thames wound its way through the Chiltern countryside. Suddenly a railway bridge loomed up and we passed under this Brunel structure. Not long after this, the Thames Path sign pointed away from the river to the adjacent tree-lined slopes. It led upwards to a path cut into the chalk hillside, parallel to the river but high above and well screened by vegetation. We seemed to be climbing steadily and we made jokes about thinking that the Thames flowed downhill, all the time aware that somewhere below us it was indeed making its long descent in its channel through the chalk hillside. Occasionally we could hear the activity of boats hidden by the trees.

After several minutes, the path suddenly deposited us on a tree-lined drive that stretched away in front of us. We followed it, only occasionally being disturbed by a car, until we joined a road that dropped down into the village of Whitchurch-on-Thames. This was familiar territory: we had come this way many times when visiting a farm shop. Cottages, houses and the occasional antique shop stand on either side of the main street, which is rather narrow for today's traffic. This road would shortly lead us to the river, but before that there was a minor diversion around St Mary's church. We went through the lychgate and then it was just a matter of following the path beside the church and past some cottages before we rejoined the road we had left only a few minutes before. Ahead was Whitchurch Bridge, the second of the two remaining toll bridges on the Thames. We knew from driving this way that only motorists pay the toll; pedestrians go free. Away over on our right we knew must be Whitchurch Lock, which is only accessible to the public by boat.

Walking over the bridge brought us to the edge of the small Thames-side town of Pangbourne. Here we had to make a big decision. Our original thoughts were that if we were tired at this point, there was easy access to Pangbourne railway station and we could break off the walk and take the short ride to Reading. The time was now moving towards mid-afternoon. We knew that Reading was quite a distance away. I calculated that it must be at least 6 miles further. After a short discussion we decided to carry on. The weather was fine and sunny and we were not desperately tired.

Having made up our minds to continue, we ignored Pangbourne and headed for the river. Beyond the bridge a wide stretch of open grassland known as Pangbourne Meadow, which is owned by the National Trust, adjoins the river. This appeared to be a popular area for the residents of the town and visitors to relax in the fresh air and indulge in the leisure activities of picnicking, jogging or just strolling and enjoying the river scenery. By now there was also plenty of movement on the river, with a variety of boats to look at. We made our way across the meadow and soon found ourselves walking along the bank of the river, passing at regular intervals other people out for a walk. We stopped to fortify ourselves with the last of the coffee from our flask and ate an apple, conscious that it might be some hours before we were able to have supper. The river was now curving round as it meandered towards Reading through the tree-dotted meadowlands.

We kept a lookout for Hardwick House, on the opposite bank, and thought we might have missed it, when it suddenly appeared, in its setting of trees and lawns rolling down to the river. The Tudor-style building is said to have been the model for Toad Hall in Kenneth Grahame's book *The Wind in the Willows,* though the claim is also made by several other desirable residences, including another Elizabethan mansion, Mapledurham House, which lay a little further along on our journey.

Mapledurham has been in the same family for centuries. Close by is the church of St Margaret's, the final resting place for generations of the lords and ladies of the house. Another interesting feature of the estate is the watermill, which was mentioned in the Domesday Book. It is the only mill on the Thames that is still working and grinding flour for sale. Apparently the name Mapledurham means 'maple tree enclosure'. The estate has had modern fame, being used as a location in the 1976 film *The Eagle Has Landed.*

The pretty Mapledurham Lock occupied our attention. It is quite close to the mill and Mapledurham House, but unfortunately there is no access across the river at this point. The lock dates back to 1777, and in 1956 it became the first powered lock on the Thames. It is recorded as being 4.4 miles from Caversham. This was definitely interesting information for us, because Caversham Bridge, close to Reading, was our destination.

Soon after Mapledurham the towpath stopped and the Thames Path diverted inland into Purley. Turning right through a field as the guidebook instructed us brought us to a track named Mapledurham Drive, which we followed to New Hill. Next we walked over a railway bridge into Hazel Road and the modern housing estate of Purley Park. The road winds up and down through the estate and we started to become worried in case we had taken a wrong turning, though it was hard to comprehend how that might have happened. We were both getting tired now and the extra burden of having to walk on roads and pavements was beginning to have its effect on us, though we were careful not to talk about it at the time. We continued past the neat houses, anxiously looking for some sort of sign to tell us we were on the right route. It came suddenly as we spied a turning on the right named Skerrit Way. Almost at the same time we noticed the Thames Path indicator. A sense of relief flooded over us.

The instructions were to follow the road until it ended and then climb up some steps. We found them without difficulty and made our way up onto the busy road we could hear but not see. This turned out to be the A329, the same road we had travelled along at Moulsford earlier in the day. We walked along the pavement for a short distance until we came to a large building, once a hotel. The sign said 'The Roebuck' but now sadly it was boarded up, either for renovation or through lack of business. We knew that Tilehurst station, with its connection to Reading, was just a bit further along the road, but at this stage we were not going to give up. We would walk the remaining distance. We turned left beside the building, as the guidebook indicated, then down and over the railway, and suddenly we were back on to the towpath, a welcome sight. Now hopefully it was a straight walk along the river into Reading. But we were not prepared for a slight shock. A sign appeared: '5 MILES TO READING'. We had not bargained for quite that distance. What about the 4.4 miles from Mapledurham Lock? We were both tired, but there was nothing to do but continue doggedly towards our destination. The path led us along the edge of the river, often with trees overhead, giving a slightly gloomy atmosphere. The bright sunshine had disappeared, leaving a rather hazy sun in a partly cloudy sky.

We walked on through the late afternoon, only occasionally meeting another person. The path seemed to drag on endlessly. After a while we were distracted by sounds on the river. When we came out into the open and were able to see more clearly, we made out teams of rowers taking part in some form of activity. As we approached Reading, the situation became clearer. The river was alive with boats. We asked an onlooker what the event was and were informed that this was a prelude to the Reading Regatta, which was due to be held shortly and for which teams were now being selected. But what was more important to us at this stage of our walk was that our destination, Caversham Bridge, was now in sight. We walked past the officials in their blazers and white trousers, the crowds enjoying the closing stages of the event, and the hamburger tents. It was with considerable relief that we finally reached the bridge. Now it was just a matter of climbing up to the road and walking the half mile or so to Reading railway station, where we could catch the bus back home.

Unfortunately, in our tiredness we took a wrong turning and actually walked further than we needed to. Even then we had to stop and ask a passer-by the way. He directed us through a nearby car park. We followed his advice and fortunately found the railway station without further difficulty.

After calling in for a comfort stop we made our way to the bus stop. We did not have to wait long before our bus pulled in, and we relaxed thankfully on the back seat as it took us home. We were exhausted, but in spite of the long day, we felt elated. We were pleased with ourselves for managing what we had set out to achieve: walking our longest section so far in a single day.

Reading To Henley-On-Thames

8.9 MILES (14.2 KILOMETRES)

After the long walk from Wallingford to Reading, we looked forward to a shorter one of just under 9 miles. The weather had been hot and sunny for most of the week and the forecast for the Saturday was for similar conditions, except that there might be the occasional rain shower. Just to be on the safe side we each packed a rain mac and overtrousers. However, as we set out to catch the first bus of the day to Reading, the morning had all the appearance of preparing for another sunny day. The bus departed at ten to seven, and there were few passengers as it made its way through places like Marlow on the way to Reading. We had intended to get off the bus in Caversham, but unfortunately we missed the stop. The driver obligingly let us out on the road to Caversham Bridge, which spans the Thames between Caversham and Reading. We walked back to the Costa coffee store we had seen from the bus, and as it was only ten to eight we expected to have to wait a few minutes until opening time. However, it was a happy surprise to find that it opened at half past seven. It proved to be a pleasant establishment with coffee to match and the availability of a comfort stop as well. We took our time over our drinks, knowing that today's walk would be short and that we could take a leisurely pace. After this welcome break, we made our way to Caversham Bridge and rejoined the Thames where we had left off on the previous walk, arriving there at just before nine.

The towpath followed the southern bank of the river, which was calm and peaceful at this time in the morning. Signs of a good day were becoming more apparent as the sun started to rise above the mist on the horizon. There were not many people about. Along this section of the river, close to Reading town centre, the riverbank is dominated by blocks of apartments and offices. After a short distance we came to the aptly named Reading Bridge, the second of the Thames bridges that serve the town. Nearby is Caversham Lock, which dates back to 1777, when £1,000 was allocated for its construction. Unfortunately, we did not see the tortoise that we read is apparently spotted from time to time in the water. This is most likely a terrapin that was released when it grew too big, during the Ninja Turtle craze of a few years ago. Next, King's Meadow appeared, a pleasant grassy area adjoining the river.

At the point where the Kennet and Avon Canal joins the Thames, a rather novel bridge ascending in a gentle curve allowed us to cross the mouth of the canal. Opened in stages between 1723 and 1810 to provide an inland access to the sea, the Kennet and Avon stretches 87 miles (140 km) to link the Thames with Bath and Bristol. Sadly, by the 1950s some sections had closed and for a few years it looked as if its usefulness had ended. Now, thanks to a dedicated group of volunteers, it has been made navigable again and was officially reopened by the Queen in 1990.

We walked along, enjoying the river landscape and taking the opportunity to use our cameras now and then. Sonning Lock was the next landmark on the river. This is a pretty lock with trees and flower beds, and, according to the various information sites on the Thames, it dates back to 1773. Sonning Bridge is only a short distance away. The current bridge, a red brick structure with no less than eleven arches, was opened in 1775, but there was a wooden bridge over the Thames here for centuries before that. A stone marker in the centre of the bridge marks what was once the dividing line between the ancient kingdoms of Mercia and Wessex and now separates the counties of Berkshire and Oxfordshire. The bridge is quite narrow and traffic is controlled by lights. We made our way up to the road and carefully crossed it to go and have a look at Sonning, which lies just a few yards from the bridge. This is a pleasant little village, but it appears to suffer from the constant flow of heavy traffic. Unfortunately, the local hostelry, The Bull Inn, was not open, but we explored the church, which has some rather nice stained-glass windows. After we had sought permission, these provided some excellent practice for camerawork. Leaving the village, we made our way carefully over the busy bridge to visit Sonning Mill. Once a working mill, it has now been turned into a well-known theatre and restaurant. We explored for a few minutes and then, having exhausted our curiosity, we returned to the bridge and towpath.

After Sonning, the Thames flows through pleasant countryside to Shiplake. As the day progressed, we saw more boats making their way up or down the river. We stopped for a while to have some lunch, watching the placid life evolving in front of us. Being on or by the river does seem to induce a pleasant feeling of relaxation. Perhaps that is why boating is so popular: it slows down the pace of life, something badly needed today.

Soon Shiplake was in sight. According to the guidebook, somewhere in the trees close by was Shiplake College. Quite a well-known school, it is young by some college standards: it was founded in 1959 in what had once been a private residence, Shiplake Court.

Shiplake Lock appeared, pretty and rural. At this time of day it was busy. We stopped for a short while to watch. There always seems to be something of interest to see when the locks are in use. One of the guidebooks indicated that there were toilets here, but when we asked the lock-keeper if we could use them, he was reluctant to let us.

Eventually he remarked that if we were desperate he would unlock one. In the end he gave us the key.

At Shiplake it was necessary to leave the river for a while and walk across a field to a lane, which led onto a minor road lined with expensive-looking houses, all of which appeared to have private access to the banks of the river. What had happened to the towpath puzzled us. The road took us past Shiplake railway station, and onto a path beside more large houses surrounded by leafy trees. One of these houses was rather interesting because there was a miniature railway wandering through its extensive garden. The small station buildings had a definite Eastern European look about them. It would have been nice to have the opportunity to view the rolling stock in action, but on this occasion all was quiet on the track. We continued on the path, with houses on one side and horses in a field on the other, and after a short distance it became clear that we were joining the river again. The path gave way to the towpath, with lush meadows on one side. Now it would be straight walking along the river into Henley, which was already in sight. By now the river was alive with activity. Pleasure craft, weekend or holiday boats passed us constantly, interspersed with the occasional smaller open boat, sometimes rowed but often under power, the owners taking friends or family out for a trip on the river. The towpath was once again attracting people, this time out for an afternoon stroll from Henley. Few looked as if they were long-distance walkers. In fact, this was one of the few days on which we had not encountered anyone else who was walking the Thames Path.

Just before Henley lies Marsh Lock, of particular interest because the footpath crosses the water on a long wooden walkway, which gives an excellent view of what is happening on the river. As we discovered, it is also a good spot for photography.

As Henley town was quite close, we stopped off for a break at the River & Rowing Museum. This is close to the towpath and it is possible to access the café without actually going into the museum itself. From the museum it was only a short walk into Henley, with its lovely bridge, built in 1786, with the church of St Mary's close by. We had already seen Henley once before, from the bus on route to Reading in the early morning to start our walk. Now we would be able to catch the same bus to take us home. Henley is a pleasant riverside town and on a Saturday afternoon it is quite busy, with local residents shopping and visitors sightseeing. We arrived at the bus stop in narrow and busy Bell Street and joined the small queue. We just had a few minutes to spare before the bus arrived. We settled back for the journey home, glad of a chance to sit down.

The shorter walk this time had been rather nice after the previous long one and once again we had experienced walking through a variety of scenery. We estimated that we must be roughly halfway to the Barrier — our ultimate destination.

Henley-On-Thames To Marlow

8.6 MILES (13.8 KILOMETRES)

The next section of the Thames Path was familiar territory. We had covered it several times before, a pleasant walk of just under 9 miles, mostly through meadows adjoining the river. After our usual early start we arrived in Henley on the first bus of the morning, with all the indications of a fine and sunny day ahead. It was the first week in July. We were fully aware that this was the week of Henley Regatta and were a little concerned about what sort of detour we might have to make, as our route lay directly through the area of the Thames used for the event; even the bus took a different route to the bus stop in the centre of the town.

We decide to have an early-morning cup of coffee before starting out. In the absence of a Costa store, we retreated to Caffè Nero, which opened earlier than we expected. It was just coming up to half past eight when we made our way down the High Street to Henley Bridge, where our walk was to begin. It was quite clear that the normal route of the Thames Path from the bridge was not available to us. Rows of large marquees now lined the banks of the river, taking up the entire length of the regatta course of 1 mile 550 yards (2,112 metres). The tents stretched as far as the eye could see, providing facilities for competitors and refreshments for the spectators. The regatta officials in their blue blazers sporting club badges were everywhere and one of them directed us between a line of tents. Great activity was going on, getting the tents ready for the crowds that would arrive a little later. A few spectators were already claiming prime positions on the riverbank.

We walked on, viewing all the preparations taking place for the day ahead, the most important of the whole event. There were stalls selling everything from hats to jewellery, not forgetting the seemingly inevitable hamburger stands. It all seemed to go on forever, and we began to wonder if the tents and stands would continue on all the way to Marlow, but as we neared the end of the regatta course they started to peter out. It is an interesting fact that the Oxford and Cambridge Boat Race, which now takes place between Putney and Mortlake, was first held in 1829 between Hambleden Lock and Henley Bridge. Henley Royal Regatta was started shortly after the loss of this attractive event to the town.

The start of the regatta course is marked by Temple Island, on which stands what looks like a Grecian temple topped by a cupola that shelters the statue of a naked woman looking down over the part of the river known as Henley Reach. The building is actually a Georgian fishing lodge or summer house, which dates back to 1771 and is part of nearby Fawley Court, one of the lesser-known stately homes of England. We had to wait until we got home to search and learn a little more about it. Apparently a manor house has stood on the site since Norman times. It was completely rebuilt around 1684, some sources claim to the design of Sir Christopher Wren, and it is believed that during the 18th century the grounds were landscaped by Capability Brown. After World War II the house was sold to the Polish Marian Fathers and run first as a school and later as a retreat and conference centre. It has recently been sold again and returned to private ownership.

Just before reaching Temple Island, walkers with a special interest in ecclesiastical buildings can divert for a few minutes to Remenham Church, which is easily accessible from the towpath. Caleb Gould, a lock-keeper at nearby Hambleden Lock from 1777, died at the grand age of 92 in 1836 and is buried in the churchyard. His epitaph reads:

This world's a jest
and all things show it;
I thought it once
and now I know it.

However, on this walk we decided to forgo the opportunity to visit the church as we were intent on reaching the open land beyond Hambleden Lock.

The river starts to make a wide curve after Temple Island, and as we looked across to the opposite bank we spotted a rather imposing house. This is Greenlands, built in 1853 by W. H. Smith of bookstore and stationer fame, who later became Viscount Hambleden.

Shortly after this landmark we reached Hambleden Lock, which is almost dwarfed by the adjoining weirs and Hambleden Mill with its distinctive weatherboarding. A mill on this site was mentioned in the Domesday Book. The last mill ceased working in the 1950s and the building is now converted into apartments.

It was while we were at Hambleden Lock that I was called to duty in another role. I had momentarily separated from Johanna, who had stopped to take some photographs of moored boats, and I had walked on to the lock. When eventually I turned to see where she was, I spotted her frantically beckoning me to come to her. It turned out that she had been talking to a couple from one of the moored boats and in the process of conversation had mentioned that my first novel, *Julie*, had just been published. The lady she was talking to wanted to buy a copy and have it signed. The author was happy to oblige.

Not far from Hambleden Lock is the only diversion from the river on this section. A leafy lane leads away and slightly upwards from the river for several hundred yards until it reaches the tiny hamlet of Aston. On the way we stopped to look at a colony of red kites who appeared to have attached themselves to a clump of trees at the edge of a small field. These magnificent birds are a wildlife success story. Reintroduced into Buckinghamshire a few years ago after complete extinction in England, they have quickly established themselves in the area and are now quite a common sight. This was the first time we had seen so many together in one place. We spent several minutes watching their beautiful flight as they seemed to glide effortlessly through the air making their distinctive whistling sound. We tried to photograph them, but it proved to be extremely difficult.

For the walker, Aston is perhaps remembered mostly for the Flower Pot Inn, but when we passed at mid-morning it was closed, so we followed the instructions in the guidebook and took a turning on the left shortly afterwards. Almost immediately we found ourselves in open country, high up above the Thames. The marked path leads directly in the direction of Culham Court, which dates back to 1771 and stands in a commanding position overlooking the river and the surrounding countryside. Although the red brick house is visible from quite a distance, close up it is almost completely hidden by high hedges.

We walked slowly past and it soon became clear that the signs were leading us back to the river. However, before we finally reached the towpath again, we had to walk through a field occupied by some cows. We marched boldly across the grass, conscious of being stared at, but the cows were more interested in securing late breakfast than in coming to inspect us.

Now we were beside the river again. Here the Thames Path route is mainly through meadows at the edge of the water. We met several other people, including a group of four women who were walking the Thames Path, again in the opposite direction to us, 'in bits and pieces' when they could. As usual we exchanged experiences and wished each other success in completing the mission. We plodded on, admiring the river scenery and the birds and waving to the occasional passing boat. The bright sky of earlier had now clouded over a little and there was a hint of rain in the air, but nothing more.

It was not long before we caught sight of Danesfield House high up on the chalk cliffs on the other side of the river. This neo-Tudor building was built between 1899 and 1901 as a private residence on the site of a previous manor. It was once home to a section of the Royal Air Force and was known as RAF Medmenham. Now it is a luxury hotel and its white exterior is a noticeable landmark from the river.

Shortly afterwards we arrived at Hurley Lock. This told us that we had covered nearly 4 miles from Hambleden Lock. The pound lock at Hurley was opened in 1773, but a river crossing here is recorded as early as 450 AD. When we arrived at the lock, late on a Saturday morning, the river was busy with craft queuing up to use it. This is certainly one of the most attractive locks we had so far encountered. There are three weirs, so its area is more spread out, inviting visitors to linger a while. A rustic bridge takes walkers over to an island on the other side of the lock, and a second returns them later to the riverbank. There is also a path to Hurley village, which is close by and worth a visit if the time is available. Many claim that it is one of the prettiest of the Thames-side villages. It predates the Norman Conquest and was know to the Danes under the name of Herlei. Part of the parish church was originally the chapel of the former Benedictine monastery, which was mentioned in the Domesday Book.

After spending some time taking photographs at the lock, we continued on our way. We knew that we were now not far from our destination. First we would have to cross the river again. This is achieved by means of a footbridge, which replaced a ferry as recently as 1989. From here it is a straight walk along the river into the town of Marlow. Bisham Abbey appears on the opposite bank of the river, though little of the original building remains; the later Tudor manor house is now a National Sports Centre. Bisham church, a well-known local landmark, is also close by and stands almost at the edge of the river.

Before we reached Marlow there was another lock to pass. Temple Lock was built about the same time as Hurley Lock. It is actually in sight of Marlow and from there we could see quite clearly the spire of All Saints' church reaching to the sky beyond Marlow Bridge.

Quite a lot of people now shared our path, including many out for a pleasant afternoon stroll. The earlier threat of rain had long since disappeared and it had become an enjoyable sunny day. The path here becomes hemmed in on both sides and as a result narrower. On one side is the river and on the other the wire fence that closes off the adjoining meadows, which often have livestock on them. Walking proved more difficult, as frequently it was necessary to step aside to make way for other people, but most passed with a smile or a few words of greeting. As we drew nearer to Marlow, the magnificent suspension bridge came into full view. This is a classic scene for photographs. The bridge was designed by William Tierney Clark after his success with the one at Hammersmith, to which it bears a strong family resemblance. Tierney Clark also designed a similar bridge that spans the Danube in Budapest. Opened in 1832, the bridge at Marlow has since had to be strengthened to meet the demands of modern living. What a blessing that they did not replace it with something more modern!

It was early afternoon when we finally walked into the tiny High Street of Marlow, which was busy with locals doing their weekend shopping and visitors sampling the amenities. Marlow is still a pleasant little riverside town that retains something of its former old-time character. The name Marlow means 'land remaining after the draining of a pool'. The George and Dragon, close to the bridge, looked inviting, so we stopped for a glass of cider. After that it was just a short walk to the bus stop. We were on home territory here, but the next leg of our walk would take us even closer to London, with the exciting prospect of what new scenery would greet us.

SECTION TEN

Marlow To Windsor

14.4 MILES (23 KILOMETRES)

After several 'short' walks, a slightly lengthier one loomed up for us on the next stage of our journey. We now embarked on these more challenging stretches with the knowledge that we were no longer strangers to walking the distances, and this gave a boost to our confidence. On top of that we were aware that we had passed the halfway mark on our journey and the question in our minds was not whether we could do it, but when we would complete it.

With a distance of over 14 miles to walk, we felt it prudent to yet again make an early start. People have asked us why we always did so. Our reply is invariably the same: it is purely a matter of choice. We both happen to be at our best in the mornings and prefer to start and finish early; for us there is something rather special and invigorating about being out and about at the start of the day. Nevertheless, those who like to make a more leisurely start can be reassured that everything we did can be achieved by setting out several hours later.

The minor heatwave of the preceding week had disappeared by the time Saturday arrived, and the forecast for the weekend was for cloudy skies and the occasional shower. There was a hint of rain in the air as we set out on foot for the bus station.

We arrived in Marlow with a few spots of rain on the windows of the bus. The bus stop was conveniently opposite the local Costa, so we

The source stone in Gloucestershire – where our long walk started from

Infant Thames – now beginning to look like a river

Ha'penny Bridge at Lechlade – the highest point on the river boats can reach

The bridge at Newbridge and the welcome end of one of the longest
sections of the route

Swinford Bridge – still a toll bridge but free for Thames Path walkers

A much larger Thames passes through Oxford

The Thames at Sonning with a pleasure boat
leaving picturesque Sonning Bridge

Goring Lock – almost halfway on our journey

The Thames near Streatley and river traffic heading downstream

A wider Thames near Marlow – with Dansfield Hotel in the background

History along the way – the Magna Carta memorial at Runnymeade

Old and new – St Mary's Church at Battersea
William Blake was married here

Albert Bridge – often claimed to be the prettiest bridge crossing the
Thames in London

HMS Belfast – with Tower Bridge in the background

The changing landscape of the Thames — Canary Wharf viewed from close
to Greenwich

The Thames Barrier — where the Thames Path and our journey ended

retreated there for an early-morning coffee. At this stage of our marathon walk, we were beginning to wonder how we would manage without the Costa or Nero coffee stores and their convenient opening hours. Again and again they provided a welcome interlude in warm pleasant surroundings before we set out on our day's walk.

After a half-hour break, we were on our way down the now-quiet High Street to Marlow Bridge and All Saints' church, where we had left off the previous week. At the church there is no immediate access to the river in the direction of London. Instead it is necessary to walk along a quiet back road for several hundred yards, passing Marlow Lock on the way. Just before reaching the road there is an interesting passageway to negotiate. The reason for the name, Seven Corner Alley, soon becomes clear. It is a succession of blind ninety-degree bends. We had to leave the road to visit the lock, but we made the short diversion because there are some striking views towards Marlow Bridge and the church.

After a short photographic session we were on our way again and soon afterwards were walking across an open grassy area back to the river. The path took us under the bridge that carries the A404, known locally as the Marlow bypass. After passing a few secluded houses, the Thames Path meanders for 3½ miles through meadows at the edge of the river. The terrain is flat, unlike that on the opposite bank, which rises steeply through dense tree cover, eventually becoming Winter Hill, well known for its views over the Thames Valley. Along the bank here are some spacious and expensive houses, one even in the form of a mock castle. Most have a convenient boathouse right on the river.

As we walked, the sky was still grey and leaden, though fortunately the rain had dried up before we started out. There were few people about, though we did stop to chat for a few minutes with an elderly gentleman from Marlow who sat contemplating the river scene, his dog sitting faithfully beside him.

As we approached a field gate, we encountered a herd of cows right up against the gate, one of them suckling her calf. After a show of insistence on our part, they all grudgingly moved a few yards away and then carried on staring at us as we walked past. The railway line that connects Marlow with the main line at Maidenhead runs along the edge of this field. At one point the two-carriage diesel train affectionately named the 'Marlow Donkey' locally hurried past and the cows lost interest in us and concentrated their gaze on the train. We continued on our way through meadows, the river flowing peacefully beside us.

A steady walk brought us to Bourne End, a favourite spot on the river for yachts. We passed the impressive clubhouse of the Upper Thames Sailing Club, and though there was not a lot going on at this time of day, it was clear from the moored cruisers and dinghies that this was a busy area of the river at times. Next we had to walk along a gravel path behind houses, which led us to an area by the river. Ahead of us we could see the railway bridge and the footbridge alongside it that Thames Path walkers must cross to the other bank of the river. A young couple with their small daughter were taking a morning stroll just as we joined the river again. They asked us where we were heading and showed great interest when we explained that we were walking the Thames Path from Gloucestershire to the Barrier. Before leaving us they wished us success in completing our project.

Crossing the river here also changes counties. Bourne End is in Buckinghamshire, and Cock Marsh, where the footbridge leads, is in Berkshire. Cock Marsh is owned by the National Trust and is 46 acres of grassland and water meadows. It has been common ground for grazing since 1272. As we walked over the bridge, we met an elderly gentleman out walking with his grandson. We chatted for a few minutes before they diverted off in a different direction from ours.

After a short distance a bend in the river brought Cookham Bridge into view. This is a rather uninteresting steel structure. At one time it was a toll bridge, and the toll house is still here, but charges were abolished by the 1950s. As we drew nearer to Cookham, we misread the instructions in the guidebook. We should have turned right into the churchyard and presumably walked around the area of Holy Trinity church. Somehow we went wrong, but fortunately we ended up roughly where we were supposed to be.

Cookham is a popular spot that attracts many visitors arriving by both river and road. The village itself dates back to at least Saxon times, and archaeological finds have indicated that the surrounding area was populated earlier still. Amongst the 17th- and 18th-century buildings are a number of pubs that reflect the former status of the village, rejoicing in traditional names such as Bel & The Dragon and The Crown. Cookham has been and still is the home of some well-known people. One of its more famous residents was the artist Stanley Spencer, who was born in a house called Fernlea, on the High Street, and found inspiration in the village. A former Wesleyan chapel is now a memorial gallery to his life and work and is open to the public. On our way out of Cookham we passed the Tarry Stone, which it is believed was used in some form of sports held in the village in medieval times. Originally it was in a different place, but now it stands in a prominent position on a corner where two roads meet.

We could not return to the river immediately after leaving the village, because the Thames Path moves inland again. It was necessary to walk along a minor road from the centre of the village and then follow a path for some distance through trees, until suddenly we were on the riverbank again. Now we were on a well-defined path separated from the river at times by vegetation, with an overhead canopy of trees. A wire fence stood between us and more open land. Looking across the river we could see nothing but a dense mass of trees rising steeply upwards from the water. However, we knew from previous trips to this area that a path stretched along the river in places and that high above the trees somewhere was the National Trust estate of Cliveden, the former home of Waldorf and Nancy Astor, which we had visited on a few occasions. Designed by Sir Charles Barry in the English Palladian

Style, the house was surrounded by magnificent formal gardens and was once the glittering hub of the rich and famous. Now it is an extremely expensive and luxurious hotel. As we walked on, the riverside cottages came into view where the political scandal of the Profumo affair took place in the 1960s.

The open fields beside us gave way to elegant houses, each standing in its own grounds – desirable riverside properties. Many of these had their own tiny landing stages, with boats moored for river trips. Eventually the towpath led us onto a riverside road, and just ahead was Boulter's Lock. Once upon a time it was called Ray Mill Lock after the Ray family who operated the mill there. We also discovered that the current name derives from 'bolter', an old English word related to the milling of flour. Richard Dimbleby, the journalist and television presenter, used to live close by on Ray Mill Island. Gone are the days when Boulter's Lock was a fashionable spot for our Victorian ancestors to visit and be seen. Today interest focuses on the restaurant here. In the early days of our marriage, we indulged in an anniversary celebration dinner here, but the restaurant has changed since then. It being close to midday, we decided to have a cider in the upstairs bar, a very pleasant room overlooking the river and its activities. In the end we spent longer taking a break than we originally intended and it was coming up to one o'clock when we resumed our walk.

After leaving the lock, the towpath changes into a kind of promenade for a short distance as it heads towards nearby Maidenhead Bridge, a rather graceful stone structure carrying the A4 over the river. The present bridge dates from 1777, but there has been a crossing here for centuries.

As we approached the bridge, the rain that had been threatening all morning suddenly arrived: fine misty rain, which nevertheless was rather wetting. It meant diving into our rucksacks for raincoats. Fortunately it was of short duration, and by the time we reached the bridge it had almost stopped. After crossing the river we turned left and then walked through a boatyard and beneath the bridge onto the towpath. Just as we emerged from under the bridge, we noticed the remains of what had clearly been a picnic on the strip of green between us and the river. A number of people were on or around a boat moored nearby; one of the more senior members of the group spied us walking and immediately expressed an interest in what we were doing. We chatted to him for several minutes and told him of our quest. It turned out that he did not live very far from us and was out for the day with his family.

By now the rain had completely disappeared and the sun shone brightly from a clear sky. We passed under Brunel's railway bridge, which was built in 1838. It spans the river on an amazing flat arch, and despite doubts over its construction by critics when it was built, it has survived the test of time and carries trains across the river every day.

Finding a spot with a nice view of Bray across the river, we stopped for a belated lunch and coffee from our flask. Unlike on our side of the river, the area around the village of Bray was quite built up, though the only thing that attracted our attention was what appeared to be a busy restaurant right at the water's edge. Bray is quite a popular and fashionable place and a number of well-known people live there. Many people of course associate it with the song about its vicar.

Suitably refreshed we started walking again, enjoying the greenery around us and watching the occasional pleasure boat moving up or down the river. It is always interesting to observe the water birds, who carry on their activities with complete disregard for the human activity around them. In fact for the most part they seem absolutely oblivious to people and passing boats, unless of course there is the chance of a titbit of food. A prime example of using the trappings of modern civilisation as much as it suits one's lifestyle.

We came up to Bray Lock in warm afternoon sunshine. Only a few boats were using the lock and we stopped to chat to the lock-keeper for a few minutes while the level of water dropped. He commented on the change in the weather from a few hours earlier. After the boats left the lock, we proceeded along the towpath, which is pleasant walking along this stretch. Soon we came to the bridge taking the M4 motorway over the Thames. What a contrast this modern structure is to Brunel's railway bridge just a few miles upstream! Not far away is a footbridge, which the guidebook describes as appearing to go nowhere. Apparently the secret is that it carries a gravel conveyor across the river. There is an interesting diversion a few yards further along. A clearly defined path will take walkers who have the time to Dorney Court, a delightful and picturesque Tudor manor house, which has been in the same family for thirteen generations. There is mention of a manor house here in the Domesday Book, though according to the guidebook the present one was built in 1440. We have made several visits to the manor and the adjoining church of St James and have found it an enjoyable experience on each occasion. Incidentally, when we looked up the origin of the name Dorney we discovered that it means 'island of bees'.

After Dorney a few changes came into the landscape of the Thames Path. Away to our left and hidden from view was the open strip of water that is Eton College rowing lake, while across the river are the famous Bray Studios, home of Hammer Film Productions in the 1950s and 1960s. The studio is still used for TV productions and events such as concert rehearsals. However, from the Thames Path side of the river the walker's eyes are drawn to the Victorian Gothic building of Oakley Court, which has appeared in a number of films. Now it is a hotel.

A bend in the river set us heading for Boveney Lock, the last we would pass before reaching Windsor. Just before the lock, the path passes the very interesting little church of St Mary Magdalene, which was built for the boatmen who worked on the Thames. From the river it looks almost isolated, but the guidebook told us that the hamlet of Boveney lies just beyond. It was tempting to spare a few minutes to have a look at the Tudor houses there, but with time now well on into the afternoon it was a pleasure we kept for another day.

Around this time we came upon something rather unusual. Across a field of high grass we spied a horse trap with two girls in it. The grass was so high that the lower part of the trap was lost to us. It was a photographer's dream and produced a feeling of almost stepping back in time. As the girls came towards us our cameras were at the ready. I did not do so well, but fortunately Johanna managed to get quite a good photograph.

Like many of the Thames locks, Boveney is very attractive, and the surrounding area is kept immaculate. This is said to be one of the busiest locks on the river, but when we passed it was relatively quiet. We stopped to take a few photographs and then went on our way.

As we walked along, it became apparent that we were passing Windsor Racecourse, which seemed to stretch for quite a long way on the opposite bank. We could not see any horses, or anything else for that matter, but there definitely appeared to be something going on, because we could hear the sound of a public address system in the distance.

After the earlier green landscape with its good covering of trees, there were now open fields to our left and houses on the horizon. Suddenly a familiar sight came into view: the unmistakable towers of Windsor Castle. I think we were both slightly relieved. It was now nearing four o'clock and, except for a few stops and breaks, we had been walking since just after eight. We were becoming a little tired and the thought of reaching our destination was more than appealing.

There was still a little way to go. We walked under the bridge that takes the main road by-passing Windsor over the river and then next was a railway bridge carrying the line from Slough that serves Windsor. We could see that it was now not far to Windsor town itself.

The guidebook informed us that we were walking into the Brocas, a broad open meadow on the edge of the town. An odd name, Brocas, but when we looked it up we discovered that it derived from a local family of nobility from the 13th century. Quite a lot of local residents were out having a stroll, though the weather had become less inviting, as the sunshine had now disappeared and the sky had greyed over.

Close to the town the instructions were to stray away from the river and follow a route that led us via a minor street into Eton. Only the Thames separates the town from Windsor. We ended our walk at the end of Eton main street, right next to the bridge that would take us across the river into Windsor for a bus home. However, being slightly weary and longing to have a sit-down, we were immediately attracted to an establishment right in front of us: a Costa store. Looking ahead to the next section of our walk, we wandered inside to check the opening times. In the end it was too much of an attraction to miss. We spent half an hour recuperating, drinking a cup of coffee and chatting over the day's events.

We then made our way into Windsor. The contrast in atmosphere was striking. All day we had enjoyed the peace and quiet of the river, but now we were suddenly plunged into crowds of tourists all eager to see the sights of the town. We had to wait for a bus at a stop on the edge of a crowded pavement, which was not pleasant. Every minute somebody seemed to jostle us as they walked past. Fortunately, we did not have too long to wait, and we settled back thankfully in the bus for the journey home.

Windsor To Shepperton

13.8 MILES (22 KILOMETRES)

With a fine day forecast for the following Saturday, we looked forward completing the next section of our journey and made our plans. As we had discovered the previous week when we returned home from Windsor, a change of buses at Slough was necessary. With the next section of the Thames Path close to 14 miles, an early start again seemed to be dictated. The problem was that there was no way of getting to Windsor by bus early in the morning. After some deliberation it became clear that we would have to travel by train via London.

Saturday morning saw us on the first train of the day from our local station. The departure time was 5.42 but it was surprising how many people were travelling even at that time. Nevertheless, there is always something unique and pleasant about taking a train journey so early in the morning.

When we arrived at London Marylebone, it was a quick journey by Underground to Paddington, where we were fortunate in catching the 6.50 for Oxford. This was earlier than we had anticipated. We left this train at Slough, and all that was necessary was to walk over to the next platform, where the train for Windsor was standing. We did not have to wait long for it to depart and the six-minute journey passed very quickly. We arrived in a Windsor bathed in sunshine and strangely quiet and pleasant without the crowds of people who would descend on it later in the day. We made our way to where we had left off the previous week and once again visited Costa for our pre-walk coffee.

Half an hour later, ready for the day ahead, we set off for Shepperton. First we had to walk back over Windsor Bridge to start walking on the opposite side of the river. Windsor Bridge is now for pedestrians only, but until quite recently it took traffic into Windsor from Eton. We can remember using the congested bridge in the 1960s. We spent some time taking photographs of the area and then commenced our walk. After passing Salter's Steamers, which advertised boat trips to Runnymede and Staines, we found ourselves on Romney Walk, which led us to Romney Lock, first passing a red brick Victorian water tower and then ambling through a boatyard. A curve in the river took us to Black Potts Railway Bridge, which carries a second railway line into Windsor. Despite its small size Windsor has two railway stations. After the bridge, the Thames Path runs beside the open space of Home Park, with its playing fields and a view of Windsor Castle. For security reasons, the area after Victoria Bridge is not open to the public, so at this point the path crosses the river. This pleasant stretch of the Thames soon brought us to Datchet, where we had to leave the river and walk along a busy road through the village. One point of interest is Old Bridge House. Apparently there was indeed a bridge here in bygone times, but it was demolished in the 1850s to make Home Park more private for Queen Victoria. Two new bridges were built to compensate for this loss to the public. One was Victoria Bridge, which we had just passed, and the second, Albert Bridge, lay ahead of us.

Thames Path walkers have to walk right through Datchet to the far end, where a sign indicates that it is time to leave the road. We skirted the edge of a field of barley, which is carefully fenced off from walkers, and rejoined the river. After a tree-lined section we suddenly came upon Albert Bridge, where we again had to cross the river. It was now comfortable walking along a quiet stretch, using a drive that led to Old

Windsor Lock. Our side of the river was clear of buildings, but the opposite bank featured some very interesting and probably expensive houses, many with their own boats at the bottom of their gardens.

With a fine day ahead, Old Windsor Lock was beginning to see activity when we arrived. Already several boats were using it. Like most of the locks on the Thames, this is an enjoyable spot to linger a while. The lock was built in 1822 and it is recorded that it cost the grand sum of £2,476. The first lock-keeper was awarded the salary of £3 10s 0d (£3.50) per month for his services. We stopped to take some photographs of the boats passing through the lock and spend several minutes chatting to an elderly gentleman who was sitting watching the activity.

After lingering for a while we continued on our way, heading for the meadows of Runnymede. In his book *Three Men in a Boat* Jerome K. Jerome describes the stretch between Runnymede and Old Windsor Lock as being a 'delightful bit of the river'. Doubtless the scenery will have changed a little since he wrote those words, but it is nevertheless still an enjoyable part of the river to walk along.

Soon after leaving the lock, the Thames Path heads along a track sandwiched between the river and a busy road. But not for long: soon the path leaves the road behind and opens up into Runnymede Meadows, where the Magna Carta was signed in 1215. This historic site was given to the National Trust by Lady Fairhaven in 1931 and is set off by the two entrance lodges designed by Sir Edwin Lutyens. Ever since I was a schoolboy and read in history lessons about the signing of the Magna Carta, I had wanted to see where it took place. The actual location has been lost in time, but a memorial is situated on a shallow rise a short walk from the river. We could not pass by without having a closer look at this bit of English history, so we carefully crossed the busy road that cuts through the meadow and made our way to the memorial, which was designed by Sir Edward Maufe and erected in 1957 by the American Bar Association. It stands in a sloping fenced-off area not far from the road – a favourite spot for tourists to take snaps, as we found out when trying to photograph the temple without anybody actually posing in front of it. Close by the domed Magna Carta temple stands the John F. Kennedy memorial of 1965, designed by Geoffrey Jellicoe, while on the tree-clad hillside above Runnymede is the Commonwealth Air Forces Memorial of 1952.

We made our way back to the river. A few minutes' walk brought us to a gate to Runnymede Recreation ground. It was a real contrast from the peaceful atmosphere we had just left to the crowded area in front of us: many parked cars, and scores of people enjoying a variety of entertainments from ball games to picnics. However, for the weary Thames Walker there is a café and more importantly – for us, at any rate – toilets.

Leaving this area the Thames Path heads for Staines, passing on the way Bell Weir Lock, said to be named after its first lock-keeper, Charles Bell. The lock dates back to 1817 and the information guide told us that the original lock-keeper's house was turned into a pub, The Anglers Rest, which apparently burnt down many years ago.

Not far from the lock we had to walk under the road bridge carrying the M25 motorway over the Thames. Traffic thunders above you as you walk underneath. After the bridge, we kept a lookout for the 'coal post'. This apparently is one of the posts set up to warn merchants bringing coal that they were crossing the London boundary and were now due to pay a levy on their cargo, as dictated by a 19th-century act.

The guidebook also tells us that on the opposite bank is a replica of the London Stone. This marked the limit of the City of London's jurisdiction over the river Thames, which lasted from 1285 until 1857, when the Thames Conservators took charge of the river.

Staines Bridge came into view. The Thames Path changes banks here, but we carried on for a short distance on the same bank into Hythe, an area of houses and riverside pubs. The word Hythe means 'landing place or harbour' and we felt we ourselves were now ready for some form of resting place for a while. We stopped off at the Swan Hotel and were a bit taken aback by the bored and indifferent attitude of the young woman who served us. Fortunately the cider was good.

Returning to our walk, we had to cross Staines Bridge and resume on the opposite bank. We were now in Staines town proper and it is recommended that walkers make a minor detour to view the town hall. It is only a minute's walk from the river and is quite an impressive building of white and yellow stone. The date 1880 is visible on its exterior. We took a few photographs and then returned to the river.

As we continued, it soon became clear that something was happening nearby. Not only was there the sound of a distant tannoy, but there was also increased activity on the river. We found ourselves walking with impressive houses on our left and Staines Regatta in full swing on our right. Sculling crews strained their utmost on the river under the watchful eye of the official's boat, while in the gardens of the houses, residents entertained friends over lunch, with a grandstand view of the proceedings. As we walked on, the unmistakable smell of the hamburger stands drifted our way. We soon entered a dense crowd of people at what was the start and finish of the regatta. However, after negotiating a very busy car park, suddenly we were on the towpath again and on our own except for occasional joggers, who seemed to be taking only a mild interest in the events taking place on the river.

From time to time a cyclist would pass us. It was noticeable that from here on the number of bicycles increased considerably. This could be due to the fact that the towpath had now become a more defined hard track and thus more suited to riding a bicycle. It has to be said that a minority of these cyclists were not really courteous to walkers. While most took care and thanked us for stepping out of their way, some appeared to consider that the towpath was exclusively for their use and rode along at great speed seemingly oblivious to any walkers on the same path, expecting them to move out of their way. It was also noticeable that none of the modern bicycles appeared to have what was termed in our youth an 'audible sound of approach'. Whatever happened to bicycle bells?

Soon we were moving into the area of Laleham. Back in the 1700s the river changed course, creating a large bend known as Penton Hook. The area became hazardous for boats whenever the river was in flood. To solve the problem, Penton Hook Lock was built in 1815. This created the adjoining Penton Island, which the guidebook told us was available for exploring. However, with still a few miles to go to Shepperton, we dismissed this option. Laleham Abbey and the village of Laleham are close by on the Thames Path side of the river for those who require refreshment at this stage or feel inclined to visit the village.

The next landmark is another fairly recent change to the river scenery, this time a concrete road bridge carrying the M3 over the Thames. From there it is a fairly short walk to Chertsey Lock and Chertsey Bridge.

Chertsey Lock opened in 1813. The area once known as Laleham Gulls is made up of shallows that, like neighbouring Penton Hook, used to cause problems for river traffic, so a decision was made to build a lock. Local landowner Lord Lucan (ancestor of the one who disappeared) claimed that the lock spoiled his view, therefore its construction was altered to accommodate his wishes.

Chertsey Bridge, a rather handsome seven-arched white stone structure, is another fine example of river engineering. The present bridge was opened in 1785, but there has been a bridge recorded here since the 13th century and no doubt there was some form of crossing before that.

After the bridge, we were once again in open meadows. On the opposite bank is the area known as Chertsey Meads. This is a 170-acre (69-hectare) landscape of water meadows and is an important habitat for birds and wildlife. One guidebook advised us that this would be the last such open space we would see on the Thames Path.

Soon after this, we could tell that we were nearing Shepperton. Trees line the route, and there are signs of a local resident population. Houseboats lined the riverbank, and many of the occupants were enjoying the late-afternoon sunshine. We stopped to talk to one young man, who told us that he and his partner had been living on their boat for two years but were shortly going to sell up and emigrate. He also told us that during World War II, barges had been moored along this stretch of the river before being deployed on the D-Day landing. With that snippet of local history, and conscious that Shepperton railway station was still some distance off, we continued on our way.

When Shepperton Lock came into view, we knew that the end of our day's journey was in sight. Shepperton Lock is another whose building was dictated by the shallows in the river in this area. A wooden lock was built to alleviate this problem in 1813; this was replaced with a stone structure in 1899. The nearby Pharaoh's Island was given to Admiral Lord Nelson after the Battle of the Nile.

This section of the Thames Path ends abruptly at the ferry landing. The guidebook directed us to turn left into Ferry Lane to find Shepperton town and its railway station. After proceeding along Ferry Lane for a short distance, surrounded by the trappings of suburbia, we were suddenly faced with a T-junction. It was clear from the direction that we had come from that the route must continue to our right. However, this section of road seemed to be endless and we began to be concerned that we were going the wrong way. There were few people about, except for those in passing cars. Then we saw a young couple walking towards us on our side of the road. They confirmed that we were correct and, now a little weary, we continued walking. It was another ten minutes before we came to Shepperton station. The ticket office was closed, so we were glad that we had planned ahead and purchased our tickets the previous day. We joined the handful of people waiting on the platform. The train arrived a few minutes later, and we were soon on our way back to London. We had completed another part of the Thames Path and we were conscious that as we moved closer to London the scenery walked through would change yet again.

SECTION TWELVE

Shepperton To Teddington

11 MILES (17.6 KILOMETRES)

After a dismal wet Saturday the previous week, it was encouraging to learn that a fine day was forecast for this one. Another early start found us on the first available train from Waterloo to Shepperton, at 7.12 a.m. One slight miscalculation on our part was to assume that there would be a toilet on the train. To our dismay we discovered that South West Trains do not consider it to be a requirement on this service. Nor is such a convenience deemed necessary at Shepperton station. Thus subdued, we made our way back along the route of our previous brief visit. I remembered that the map showed toilets in Shepperton High Street. I just prayed that it was not one of those that did not open until the shops started business. Luck was on our side, because the toilet (there was only one) was one of those stainless-steel affairs that need money to open the door. I held my breath as I inserted the 20p required. After what felt like an excessive delay, the door slid open. It did much for our mental and physical comfort.

Thus relieved, we set about the major task of the day: the walk to Teddington. There is no Costa or Nero store at Shepperton and at that time in the morning nothing else was open that might provide any refreshment. It was the first time this had happened to us, but as we always carried a flask it was not a major problem.

At Shepperton there are two different ways to start the next section of the Thames Path. The walker can either take the ferry across the river or walk an alternative route. As the ferry did not start operating until around nine and it was now just after eight, the decision was made for us.

At first the path is clearly defined across a small car park and then continues along the edge of some public gardens. Suddenly it ends up on the edge of the river. This is not, however, the main stream. At Shepperton the Thames twists and turns, so a new section was cut to straighten out the route for river traffic. This is known as Desborough Cut and this is the section walkers follow if they cross to the opposite bank by means of the ferry. The alternate route we had opted to take follows the path of the old loop, but most of it is out of sight of the river.

This meant that our meeting with the Thames here was extremely brief. After walking past a few moored boats we had to turn off into a wooded area. The path is not very well marked at this stage and several times we began to wonder if we had gone wrong. However, eventually we joined the road we had been guided to, so everything was all right.

We passed several hotels and then the instructions were to turn off the road and head towards a white weather-boarded cottage. We found this without difficulty and crossed the grass in front of it to find the lane that would lead us to Walton Bridge and the river. We found the lane, but, in the absence of any Thames Path signs, we had to guess which way to turn. Our decision proved to be correct: a few minutes' walking brought us to what could be no other than Walton Bridge and the very busy pedestrian crossing mentioned in the guidebook. We crossed safely using the island in the centre of the road and then made our way over the bridge. This is the point at which the two routes of the Thames Path out of Shepperton meet up.

Once back on the security of the path beside the river, we started to enjoy the morning and the comparatively peaceful atmosphere after the busy road we had just encountered. Walking along the river one sees very little of the town of Walton itself, though we knew that we were on the edge of it. Quite elegant properties decorated the opposite bank, and several industrial units were a reminder that civilisation was not far away. However, the presence of a few boat marinas emphasised the river's role as a place of recreation.

This was quite a pleasant stretch of the river. We passed the old lock-keeper's house, standing forlornly on its own on a leafy section of the river. Today there is little trace of the former lock on the quiet stretch of water. The date on the house is 1812. This was no doubt the date the first lock was built, but it did not have a very long life: a new one was built downstream in 1856. Just by the old lock house is a footbridge that leads to Sunbury Ait, an island between this section of the river and the weir beyond. Many of the islands on the Thames are known as aits or eyots. This particular island is uninhabited and is a haven for wildlife. We watched a heron close to the opposite bank, apparently resting after early-morning fishing. Unfortunately, as so often happens with birds, it flew off just as we were about to photograph it.

About this time the guidebook tells walkers to keep a lookout for Sunbury church with its distinctive tower and cupola. We could see it in the distance, quite unmistakeably.

We came quickly to Sunbury Lock, which was starting to get busy with river traffic. Unusually, two locks were built side by side here at different times; a second one was constructed in the 1920s, and the earlier one is rarely used now. This is the point on the river at which the Queen's Swan Uppers commence their annual count of the swan population. This event usually takes place in July.

After leaving Sunbury Lock, the towpath becomes bounded on the land side by high banking. This is the edge of Molesey Reservoirs. The bank stretches for some distance, obscuring the view. The guidebook describes this section as being claustrophobic. We did not experience it as that bad, but perhaps that was because it was a bright sunny morning. Some distance further along, we caught a glimpse of Sunbury Court on the opposite bank. This is a fine 18th-century mansion, for many years owned by the Salvation Army. From our side of the river it was partly concealed by the bungalows lining the riverbank. One item of interest we passed on this stretch was a number of huge concrete blocks on the towpath. Apparently these are another remnant from the 1939–45 war. They were intended to be part of London's anti-tank defences.

We were beginning to encounter a lot of people now, some jogging, some clearly out for a walk, and a number with dogs, and of course the inevitable cyclists who zoomed up and down the towpath. Suddenly the path opened up onto a rather nice grassy area. The guidebook advised us that this was part of Hurst Park Racecourse, once a popular venue. The course was first laid out in 1890, but, sadly for racegoers, the land was sold for building in 1962. The houses that form a backdrop to the strip of grass bordering the river are the evidence of that decision.

The grass, with the occasional tree for sitting under, looked extremely inviting. It had now turned eleven, and as we had had an extremely early breakfast we decided to stop for lunch. One of the things we had discovered walking the Thames Path was that it is often prudent to take a break when the opportunity presents itself, particularly when the route ahead is unknown.

It was a good half-hour before we resumed our walk with a slightly lighter rucksack and an almost empty thermos flask.

One notable landmark ahead of us now was the very narrow tower of Hampton church. Much closer, near to the opposite bank of the river, is Garrick's Ait and the little temple built by the actor David Garrick close to the villa he lived in. A short distance further on we came to Molesey Lock, which is almost at Hampton Bridge. There are toilets here: a blessing for the long-distance walker. We availed ourselves of this facility; we had learnt on the Thames Path to make use of such conveniences when they appeared, never being quite sure when the next one would present itself, though most writers of guidebooks do mention them.

After leaving the lock we had to walk up onto Hampton Bridge and then cross a busy road to reach Hampton Court Palace, where the walk continues. While we were at the palace we hit upon the idea of having some further refreshment, and, not being sure whether we would have to pay the entrance fee to the building in order to do so, we made enquiries of an official. He assured us that entry to the café was free and directed us there. Crowds of visitors were thronging the palace and grounds, and the café was packed. A quick glance through the door convinced us to abandon the idea of stopping for a drink. We wandered back in the direction of the river and rejoined it a few hundred yards below Hampton Bridge. It was a classic scene and we both spent a few minutes capturing the view with our cameras.

The route from Hampton Court encourages a leisurely pace. We walked more slowly, taking in the scenery before us: the activity on the river and the sought-after properties lining the route. A few people were walking along or just sitting, enjoying the view in the warm afternoon sunshine.

From here it is a pleasant walk along the river to Kingston. It did not seem too long before Kingston Bridge came into view, a very graceful and picturesque structure faced with Portland stone. There has been a bridge across the river here for centuries, but the present one dates back to 1828. It has been widened and worked on a few times since then. It carries the extremely busy A308 through Kingston, and in 2005 it was estimated that 50,000 vehicles a day crossed it.

At the bridge, Thames Path walkers have to cross the river again. We left the towpath and walked up the slope to the road. We had to walk along to a crossing and wait a few minutes before we could make our way safely to the other side, where the sign on the John Lewis department store beckoned invitingly. We were sure that some form of refreshment would be available there. We were not disappointed: the entrance from close to the bridge placed us nearly in the right position for The Place to Eat. It proved to be a good choice and, surprisingly for a Saturday afternoon, was not too crowded. We found a nice spot overlooking the bridge and indulged in a coffee and a piece of cake, confident that we would soon walk off any extra calories.

After a well-earned half-hour break we made our way down to the riverside again and continued along the path, eventually walking under a railway bridge and then coming to a park-like area. This is Canbury Gardens, which have been here since Victorian times. They seemed to be full of local people, and we were glad to escape to the other end and find more peaceful surroundings. The gardens end on a minor road, with houses on one side and the river on the other. There is no footpath on the riverside, so we were obliged to use the pavement in front of the houses. The inconvenience was of short duration: soon we came to the Half Mile Tree, as the guidebook predicted. An intriguing name, but the nearby plaque explains all. Apparently an ancient elm stood on the site until sadly it had to be removed in 1951, to be replaced by a new tree the following year. The notice does not explain where the half-mile is measured from – perhaps Kingston.

Once back on the Thames Path proper our progress to Teddington was quite rapid.

The path stretched out ahead of us, taking up the riverbank and providing an easy and pleasant walk. It was quite rural and it was hard to believe that we were close to London. From time to time we passed local walkers. We stopped to chat with one woman who was from London. She gave us details of a café in Richmond, close to the bridge, which she had found very appealing, and we made a note for the next leg of our walk. Disconcertingly, we were again interrupted from time to time by cyclists who rode furiously along the pathway, sometimes two abreast, at speeds that were in no way compatible with the location.

A few of them appeared to expect pedestrians to dodge out of their way. Perhaps a speed limit should be imposed.

Teddington Lock came into sight, and the footbridge that would take us across the river into Teddington. The bridge is actually in two parts, linked by an island: the first is an iron girder affair, and the second is a more graceful suspension bridge. As we walked across, we could see the extent of Teddington Lock. This is the longest lock on the river Thames and there are actually three locks in this complex, the first of them built in 1811. The lock has played its part in recent history, being used as the assembly point for the flotilla of small ships and boats from the Thames that went across to Dunkirk to evacuate stranded troops in 1940. Reaching Teddington gave us a major sense of achievement after all our previous days of walking: we had now reached the fringe of London. Beyond Teddington Lock the river Thames becomes tidal and the Port of London Authority takes over the administration of the river from the Environment Agency.

Once over the footbridge, it did not take us long to reach Teddington High Street, a fairly short road that still retains a small-town atmosphere. We had a fairly good idea of how to get to the railway station, but just to be on the safe side I stopped a traffic warden and asked him to confirm where it was. He assured us that we were heading in the right direction, and after turning off the main street into a side road, we found the sleepy station without any difficulty. It was actually on the same railway line that had taken us to Shepperton earlier in the day. A train for Waterloo was scheduled for 15.59, and that gave us five minutes for a welcome rest on one of the station seats. The train arrived on time, and we set off on the first part of our journey home via London.

Teddington To Putney (Southern Route)

11.4 MILES (18.2 KILOMETRES)

We were now faced with a decision: which route of the Thames Path to take through London. At Teddington there are two choices: the walker can either follow the path along the north side of the river, or travel on the south bank. We had a quick glance through the guidebook and decided that the southern route might be especially interesting.

With fine summer weather and a decision made, on Saturday 15th August we once again took the early train to London, where we made a quick Underground transfer to Waterloo. We had one bonus now with our travel arrangements. When I went to our local railway station the previous day to purchase tickets, I naturally enquired about a ticket from Waterloo to Teddington. The ticket office clerk pointed out that we did not need special tickets: our London Travelcards would take us there. Having had bad experiences in the past, and still with doubt in my mind, when we reached Waterloo I looked for an agreeable ticket inspector. I found one at the ticket barrier and he confirmed that our tickets were indeed valid to Teddington. It was, he said, 'a borderline case', and I was happy with that. It looked as if our 7.12 train was going to be delayed, but it was signalled on the departure board just 4 minutes before it was due to leave.

We arrived at Teddington shortly before eight o'clock and walked the short distance to the main street. We had made a slight miscalculation in the Costa opening time and arrived to find it still closed. Rather than wait, we went to Starbucks. After a brief coffee and comfort stop, we returned to Teddington Lock Footbridge. The weather was cool and grey, but fine sunny weather was forecast for later. Once over the footbridge we turned onto the towpath and walked past the locks, which were quiet and peaceful at this time in the morning. The ducks and geese were making the most of having the area to themselves. How busy the lock can become at times was evident from the vast number of boats tied up in the vicinity.

Our way lay along a pleasant gravel path, with the river on one side and a wall of greenery on the other. The vegetation concealed the adjacent Ham Lands, an area of grass and scrubland created from reclaimed gravel pits and now a nature reserve. We passed the obelisk marking the point where the river is taken into the care of the Port of London Authority from the Thames Conservancy. From this point the river is tidal. Ham House soon comes into view, standing majestically a short distance from the river. As National Trust members we had visited this property on a previous occasion and found it to be an enjoyable experience. First built in 1610, it is claimed to be one of the best examples of a 17th-century mansion. The house contains some fine furnishings and there is a well laid-out garden. The Duke and Duchess of Lauderdale lived there, and the house is said to be haunted by the ghost of the duchess and her dog.

Nearby is Hammerton's Ferry, which has a regular service to the opposite bank, though every time we have been in this area we have missed seeing it in operation. On the opposite side of the river stands Marble Hill House, built in the 1720s for Henrietta Howard, Countess of Suffolk and mistress of King George II. A Palladian villa with a distinctive white exterior, it is set in 66 acres of parkland and is now owned by English Heritage.

We were approaching Richmond. A signpost on our right pointed to Petersham. According to the guidebooks, both the village and the parish church of St Peter's are well worth looking at. We debated whether to make the recommended visit, but in the end, conscious that today we had quite a long walk ahead of us, we put it off until a later date.

The scenery suddenly opens up onto Petersham Meadows, a lush green area bordering the river. Beyond lie the slopes of Richmond Park. Topping the high rise of the landscape of Richmond is the Star and Garter home for the military. This charity was founded in 1916 to help disabled soldiers from the battlefields of World War I. A hotel once stood on the site, but it was demolished and replaced by the present building. Each window facing the Thames must have a magnificent view of Petersham Meadows and the river.

We walked on, with only a wire fence between us and the meadows, where cows were placidly grazing, mostly concerned with their own activities though occasionally one nearer to us would look up inquisitively. From here there was an excellent view of Richmond Bridge. There were quite a few people on the path, most of them clearly local residents out for a morning walk with a dog, or younger people jogging. Today the numerous cyclists of the two previous walks appeared to be missing; in fact, from this point on they tended to diminish.

A little further on we had to walk inland for a short distance, as it is no longer possible to follow the edge of the river at this point. The path diverts through a grassy area, passing toilets (which we noticed were closed) and the three-arch grotto that leads to an underpass to Terrace Gardens and up to Richmond Hill. We had been up there on a previous visit to Richmond.

As we returned to the riverfront and approached Richmond Bridge, we remembered Tide Tables, the café recommended to us on our previous walk. It was easy to find, as it is right on the path and occupies the space beneath one of the arches of the bridge. Though it is quite a small establishment, there are plenty of seats outside where patrons can sit and have refreshment and enjoy a view of the river. Richmond Bridge is an impressive Portland stone structure. Dating to the 1770s, it was the eighth bridge to be built in what is now Greater London and has the distinction of being the oldest surviving bridge in the city, though it has been widened for modern traffic. We lingered a while over our coffee, supplemented with an enormous piece of cake, and thus fortified resumed our walk.

Just after Richmond Bridge are a number of interesting historical features, a feast for those inclined to wander off the Thames Path walk and explore. Local history reveals that Richmond was once a popular place for royalty to live. Within a few steps of the towpath, the guidebook told us, lie Trumpeters' House, which dates back to the early 1700s, and the Palladian villa Asgill House, which was built in the 1750s; both are on or close to the site of the Palace of Shene, built for King Henry VII. The area of Richmond was known as Shene or Sheen at the time, and the name Richmond came into use due to Henry's title of Earl of Richmond. Queen Elizabeth I died at the palace. We did not investigate, but apparently today only a few bits of the palace remain standing. Richmond Green is also in the vicinity. All points of interest, perhaps too time-consuming for the Thames Path walker with a few miles still to cover, but, for a day out exploring, Richmond has quite a lot to offer, including Richmond Park. We once did a seven-mile walk all round it, on a bright frosty December day.

The path ahead is interrupted by first a railway bridge and then a road bridge. Richmond Lock, which follows soon after, incorporates a footbridge to the opposite bank, so it is possible for walkers to change over to the other side of the river here if they wish. This is the last chance to do so until Kew Bridge. Richmond Lock is not the most attractive of locks; however, it was not built in 1894 for its beauty, but to do the essential job of controlling the level of water upstream from Richmond towards Teddington. It is under the control of the Port of London Authority.

After the lock, we found ourselves walking along the edge of the Old Deer Park, now turned into playing fields and a golf course. It is home to Kew Observatory, built so that King George III could pursue his hobby of astronomy. Apparently the obelisks in the grounds were set up to assist him in observing the passage of Venus in 1769.

While we were trying to spot the observatory through the screen of trees, our attention was drawn to the opposite bank of the river. First we saw Isleworth Ait, and then the vista of Old Isleworth opened up, with the church providing a landmark. Next to Isleworth is the 200-acre Syon Park and Syon House, the London home of the Duke of Northumberland and his family. The map shows that just beyond Syon Park are the remains of the once-busy Brentford Dock. Somewhere around that point the Grand Union Canal meets the Thames. We thought we could see what would be the meeting point.

Looking at the map, we realised that we were actually following a wide curve of the river as it bends round in the direction of Kew Bridge: such changes of direction are not so obvious to someone walking on the riverbank. The many trees on our right and the glimpses of parkland made it clear that we were now at the edge of Kew Gardens. Only the towpath and a fence separate the gardens from the river. We had both been impressed with the rural nature of the walk from Teddington so far. It was hard to imagine at this stage that we were within the boundary of London. Here at Kew we were brought into contact with a few more people, some of them locals but the majority obviously out for the day. We passed a busy car park. At one point we could see quite clearly into the gardens and make out the red brick of Kew Palace. This was built by Samuel Fortrey, a merchant of Dutch extraction. In its early life it was apparently known as the Dutch House. The building was purchased by King George III in 1781 and converted into a royal palace. On a previous visit to Kew Gardens we had been inside.

The graceful arches of Kew Bridge were now right in front of us. Looking at some of the older bridges spanning the Thames, we were always impressed with the design and work that must have gone into creating such elegant and picturesque structures. The modern concrete bridges, we feel, are no comparison. This is the third bridge to be built at Kew and it is comparatively modern, having been opened by King Edward VII and Queen Alexandra in 1903. At the time it was named the King Edward VII Bridge, but apparently the name was not very popular and reverted to Kew Bridge.

It was now long past midday and the need for food and a comfort stop was well advanced. At first it looked as if it was going to be difficult to find somewhere to sit. There were not many opportunities at this point along the path. However, with family history and numerous visits to the National Archives at Kew at the back of my mind, I automatically set off in that direction. It took us about seven minutes to walk along a pathway that I knew would bring us close to the building. We discovered to my relief that the green area round the building was sparsely occupied by people, and we ate our lunch sitting at one of the picnic tables there. Since I was the holder of a reader's card for the archives, I felt sure there would be no objection if we used the toilets inside the building.

Once on the road, or rather footpath, again, we resumed our pace towards Chiswick, the next settlement along the route. After leaving Kew Bridge, we passed quite a few blocks of buildings bordering the river, some of them relatively new. Across the river, which at this point is quite wide, the bank is lined with what are often described as 'desirable' properties, in an area known as Strand on the Green. Though we felt slightly envious of the people living there, we did wonder what happens when the river floods, as most of the houses are not very high above the water.

Chiswick Bridge came into sight. Quite an elegant reinforced concrete structure, faced in Portland stone, it carries the A316 road across the river. Compared to some of the other bridges across the Thames, it is quite a youngster. It was opened in 1933.

Shortly afterwards we came to Mortlake, though all the Thames Path walker sees of it is the bit that borders the river. The Ship Inn is dwarfed by Mortlake brewery, which stands on the riverbank. The smell of hops filled the air as we walked past. Apparently beer has been made here for centuries, but we read that like many factories it has been faced with closure.

Barnes Railway Bridge is the next landmark along this stretch of the river. Constructed from girders, it replaced a similar bridge in 1895. Barnes is one of the few bridges in London that have a footbridge incorporated into the structure, though when we were there it was closed for repairs. At this point the towpath ends and we had to walk along the road that runs alongside the river. This was not a problem: in fact, it is rather pleasant with the river on one side and rows of Georgian houses on the other. This is a well-known part of Barnes, known simply as The Terrace. It is also Blue Plaque country. The composer Gustav Holst lived in one of the houses, and Dame Ninette de Valois, founder of the Royal Ballet, in another.

The road continues along the riverside for a short distance. The older houses are gradually replaced by more modern residences. Barnes must be a pleasant place to live, and this is reflected in the fact that quite a lot of well-known personalities reside here.

It was now low tide, and mudflats were exposed at the edge of the river. Water birds were making the most of this opportunity and were foraging for food in the mud. From time to time we spotted cormorants resting on any available perch, drying their feathers.

Suddenly the towpath returned and we said goodbye to Barnes. Now we were heading for Hammersmith, following another great curve in the river. The map shows disused reservoirs situated to our right, and according to the guidebook some of these have been put to good use and turned into a nature reserve. Once again we commented on how hard it was to believe that we were in London.

Hammersmith Bridge loomed up ahead of us, a grand ornate Victorian suspension bridge that was opened in 1887. Designed by Sir Joseph Bazalgette, it replaced another suspension bridge designed by William Tierney Clark, whose work we had come across at Marlow, earlier on our Thames Path walk. Doubtless there was some form of crossing before that. This is a busy bridge, which carries the A306 out of London. There is also a walkway across the river.

Just beyond Hammersmith Bridge we passed Harrods Depository, another well-known landmark. This striking red and orange building was built in 1894 as a warehouse and furniture depository for the Knightsbridge store. The name is still proudly displayed in large letters on the top of the building, though the building has now been turned into expensive residential apartments.

The next area we came to is known as Barn Elms. Again these are old reservoirs that have been turned into wetlands for water birds, some of them quite rare. There is a visitor centre close by and the guidebook recommends a visit but suggests that a whole day is needed to digest everything. Leaving this as yet another pleasure for the future, and as we were feeling slightly tired, we pressed on to Putney, which we knew could not be far away now.

Almost without warning, the towpath ended. Instead a kind of promenade stretched ahead of us to Putney Bridge. We knew that we were saying goodbye to the towpath for good. From now on, the Thames Path route would be a different experience as we walked through London.

For the present, there was almost a 'seaside' feeling as we walked along the promenade, with the wide river on one side and numerous boat clubs on the other. Slipways lead into the river here, emphasising the importance of Putney for boating.

We arrived at Putney Bridge, busy on this Saturday afternoon. We knew we had to look for a bus stop so that we could catch a bus into central London. After the peace and tranquillity of the day so far, it was a shock to encounter the crowds of people in the High Street. Eventually we found a bus stop that indicated that the no. 74 bus bound for Baker Street stopped there. We did not have to wait long before one came along. We climbed the stairs to the upper deck and sank gratefully into a seat for the journey to Marylebone Road. From there it would be a two-minute walk to the railway station and a train home. Our first day of walking the 'tidal' Thames had been strikingly surprising. Instead of the concrete jungle we had anticipated, the route had been almost rural. The next section would take us through central London, and that would be different yet again.

Putney To Tower Bridge (Southern Route)

9.8 MILES (15.7 KILOMETRES)

Another fine August Saturday arrived and once again we set forth on our quest. There now remained only two sections of the Thames Path to complete, and we were feeling elated with what we had achieved. Despite all the pre-walk concerns, we had no doubts now that we would complete the 184 miles and arrive at the Barrier.

Leaving early, we made our way back to Putney. I had checked on the internet and discovered that a Costa store was located in the High Street. We got off the bus as soon as it left Putney Bridge and entered the High Street. We later discovered that we could have remained on it until the next stop. However, just after half-past seven found us in the welcoming Costa, drinking an even more welcome coffee from one of their large cups.

We took our time over the coffee and then retraced our steps to the start of Putney Bridge and St Mary the Virgin church, where the next section of the walk began. Circling round the church dwarfed by a modern building brought us to the edge of the river and a magnificent view of Putney Bridge in the early-morning sunlight. This was too good an opportunity to miss and we spent some time with our cameras, much to the interest of two young men who were sitting nearby. We chatted to them for a few minutes and then proceeded on our way.

Our contact with the river was brief. The path ended abruptly and the instructions were to turn inland and walk along Deodar Road, a quiet street lined with solid Victorian family houses. We passed the footbridge across the river, convenient for residents as it saves a walk to Putney Bridge, and then followed the road to its end. Here the way ahead was clearly marked, on a footpath leading into Wandsworth Park and back to the river. A broad path took us along the edge of the park, a favourite spot for joggers, it seemed, as several passed us with a breathless 'Good morning'. The interlude in the park did not last long. The path passes in front of an apartment block and then comes another brief detour away from the river. The guidebook is needed here as the route follows several roads before returning to the river. The roads have interesting names: Point Pleasant, Osiers Road, Enterprise Way. At the end of the last one we came to a footbridge over Bell Lane Creek, a branch of the river Wandle. The Wandle was one of the busiest of rivers in Victorian times and became heavily polluted as a result, but the bit that we crossed was just an abandoned creek opening into the Thames. Johanna spent some time trying to photograph a heron who was wading in the muddy water. Unfortunately, like most of the water birds we encountered on our walk, he was too busy doing his own thing to waste time posing for photographers.

There is a waste transfer station just a short distance further on and it is necessary for Thames Path walkers to use the road that leads past it. The guidebook recommends proceeding with care, and we could see why. On a Saturday morning the area was relatively quiet, but it was easy to see how busy it would be on a weekday. There are plans to allow the Thames Path to proceed on an overhead walkway nearer the river, but it is not in use yet. In the meantime walkers have to dodge turning lorries.

Just past the transfer station the route led us back to the river along

Nichols Walk and then past Riverside West, a modern development of apartments with a few shops and restaurants.

Wandsworth Bridge was now ahead of us. Compared to Richmond or Putney Bridge it is a dull affair with its blue and grey painted steel panels. It is another quite young bridge, only being opened in 1940 and replacing an earlier bridge.

Our return to the river was of short duration. We had to divert once again. A turn right and then another quick left brought us into a narrow section of street hemmed in by buildings, but in another half a minute we were at the Ship Inn, standing on a corner. Originally a watermen's inn, the building displays Victorian origins, but in fact it is older than that, dating back to 1786. It appears to have exploited its location and origins and is now a popular spot to visit, with a garden facing the river. We would have liked to sample its hospitality, but it was far too early in the day for it to be open.

The street names around here are interesting and perhaps reflect the history of the vicinity. We noticed Jews Row and Smugglers Way.

The Thames Path is clearly marked at this stage and we followed the road to the approach to Wandsworth Bridge. This brought us out into a busy area teeming with traffic. We noticed what looked like Wandsworth bus garage, but our task now was to cross the busy road, which we achieved with the help of the pedestrian-crossing lights. Now the instructions were to make our way along York Road, fortunately only a short distance, because it is not designed for pleasurable walking.

Juniper Drive took us back to the river, where expensive high-rise apartments overlook the water. The Thames Path follows a wide walkway at the foot of the buildings, with first-class views of the river. The development has the impressive name of Plantation Wharf. We passed what was once the site of Price's Candle factory, of which no trace remains. Apartments now occupy this area. There were not many people about close to the river, apart from the occasional jogger, or a local resident who had clearly been out shopping. All hurried on their way, most of them only briefly acknowledging our greeting. We did stop to talk to one elderly gentleman from the North of England who was visiting relatives in the area and was out for a stroll.

After another brief interlude with the river, a wide walkway with globe lighting took us back to the road again. Then it was a short walk past Battersea Heliport before returning to the river. There is a slight detour to walk under the railway bridge and then the river vista opens up again. Across the water we could see the abandoned Lots Road Power Station, but closer to hand and right in front of us the path was bringing us to a little photographic gem: St Mary's church, Battersea. It is a remnant of old London, and the present building has served the local community since 1777, yet there was a church on the site long before that. William Blake was married here. Today it is dwarfed by the high-rise developments surrounding it, yet it is not difficult to imagine how it looked and the role it played when it was part of a Thames-side village. We spent several minutes taking photographs.

We left the churchyard and continued to walk along the edge of the river, shaded by lofty blocks of apartments. The walkways alongside the river are quite pleasant on this section. One of them has the grand title of Montevetro.

On the approach to Battersea Bridge the walkway becomes wider, and just before the bridge there is a sculpture by John Ravera called *In Town*, which depicts a man and a woman holding a child aloft. We took the obligatory photograph.

We had to cross the road at Battersea Bridge. Fortunately there are pedestrian crossings, as it is very busy. The present bridge, designed by Sir Joseph Bazalgette, was opened in 1890 and replaced an earlier bridge. It is a navigation hazard at times, due to the bend of the river, and on more than one occasion has been struck by ships passing through and had to be closed for repairs.

Once over the bridge we went down the steps to the riverfront. Here was another surprise. A sculpture of two swans taking flight greeted us. It was an unusual find, and against the backdrop of the bridge it earned another photograph.

We were now on what looked like a relatively new walkway called Albion Riverside Promenade. Once again tall buildings took up the scenery on our right, but this was well compensated for by the wide expanse of the river to our left. It was surprising how many boats were going to and fro. Scarcely a minute went by when there was not some form of activity on the water. It was interesting to observe that here in London the boats that passed were mainly working boats of one kind or another, hurrying about their business.

Albert Bridge was the next bridge across the river. This is claimed by many to be the prettiest bridge in London. It is quite an impressive suspension bridge, though since its opening in 1873 it has had to be modified several times to strengthen it. It has a notice on it telling troops from the nearby Chelsea Barracks to break step when crossing it. The first bridge across the river in this area was built in the 18th century to, as one guidebook put it, 'link Industrial Chelsea with Farming Battersea'.

Here again we had to cross the road just before it goes over the bridge. This proved to be not too difficult. On the other side the greenery of Battersea Park opened up in front of us. This 200-acre (83-hectare) expanse of parkland was laid out in the 1850s and occupies reclaimed marshland and market gardens that once served London. It is a marvellous green area in South London and is well used, not only by local residents, but also by visitors to some of its attractions.

There are several paths through the park, but we chose to keep close to the river and followed a broad walkway that divides the trees from the water. We met an elderly couple out for a walk and chatted to them for a few minutes. The man had recently had a hip operation and this walk was a regular part of his rehabilitation. Along this route, we could not help but stop and spend a few minutes gazing in wonderment at the Peace Pagoda, one of a number built around the world by the Nipponzan Myōhōji Buddhist Order. It is a magnificent structure over 100 feet (30 metres) high, with wind chimes and golden statues of Buddha. Just past the Peace Pagoda are very convenient toilets, a facility we availed ourselves of.

On the edge of the park is Chelsea Bridge. Less ornate than its neighbour Albert Bridge, it is also much younger, having replaced an earlier bridge in 1937.

At Chelsea Bridge there is a major diversion to the Thames Path. The huge complex of Battersea Power Station has to be circumnavigated. This listed building with its distinctive four chimneys has stood unused since electricity ceased to be generated there in 1983. Various uses have been proposed, but as yet none have materialised. It stands stark and open to the sky. The detour we had to make to avoid the site was one of the most difficult bits of the walk so far. To start off with, we did not find the signposting of the Thames Path very easy to follow, though this may have been because we accidentally left Battersea Park by a wrong exit. Most of the route is along pavements on busy roads; one of them rejoiced in the name Prince of Wales Drive, but to get to it we had first to navigate Queen's Circus. We then walked under the bridge that carries the railway lines into Victoria station, and a few minutes later we made another discovery when we passed a quite inconspicuous doorway that bore the name Battersea Dogs and Cats Home. Almost immediately afterwards another familiar name appeared: New Covent Garden Market. We complimented ourselves on the fact that we now knew where two famous establishments are situated.

We were now in the area of London known as Nine Elms. 'Why Nine Elms?' might be the question asked. It was one we pondered over and eventually looked up. Apparently, as the name suggests, it is derived from trees. In the 17th century there was a lane here that took its name from a row of nine elms that lined it. The trees have disappeared, as seemingly has the locomotive works that once occupied part of the area.

After walking along rather drab streets, it was some relief to eventually see the Thames Path sign pointing in the direction of the river. It was now long past midday, and we were both beginning to feel the pangs of hunger. When we reached the walkway along the river again, we stopped and sat on a rather tatty bench to have a drink and some food. A few people passed and gave us curious looks. They were definitely not walkers, but just local residents going to or returning from Saturday-morning shopping expeditions and most of them did not seem inclined to want to speak; quite a contrast to the people we met on the early stages of walking the Thames Path.

Suitably refreshed, we continued along a rather functional walkway beside the river. The scenery on this stretch is not very inspiring, consisting mainly of tall apartment blocks or offices. At one point we came upon a bas-relief panel by Stephen Duncan portraying an unusual Father Thames doing battle with various sea monsters.

After another brief detour onto the road, we were back at the riverside. Ahead of us stood Vauxhall Bridge, distinctive and dominant in its red paint. It carries the A202 over the river and links Vauxhall with Westminster. Opened in 1906, it replaced the earlier Regent Bridge, which, like many on the Thames, started life as a toll bridge and occupied the site of a former ferry.

After Vauxhall Bridge the well-known landmarks of London started to appear in abundance. We continued to walk along a wide footpath, almost immediately passing the green and cream modern SIS building, headquarters of MI6. The landscape inland is dominated again by apartment and office blocks. On the other side of the river the Tate Gallery can be seen. The walkway becomes Albert Embankment, and from now on the number of pedestrians we encountered gradually increased. Nevertheless this is a pleasant part of London for walking.

Lambeth, the next bridge across the Thames, is a not unattractive steel five-arch structure. It, too, replaced a previous bridge and dates from 1932, when it was opened by King George V and Queen Mary.

We walked under it, and the panorama of tourist London opened up before us. Ahead on the opposite bank were the Houses of Parliament, Westminster Bridge was close by, and in the distance we could see the London Eye. However it would be a bit more walking before we would get a close-up of these landmarks.

After Lambeth Bridge, the first encounter of note is the Tudor brick expanse of Lambeth Palace. This has been the historic home of the Archbishop of Canterbury since the 12th century. The gatehouse with the Great Hall behind can be clearly seen. Nearby is St Mary-at-Lambeth, the former parish church. It was deconsecrated in 1972 and now houses the Garden Museum, founded by the Tradescant Trust.

We were now in sight of the Houses of Parliament and of course Big Ben, though strictly speaking the name refers to the bell, not the clock. On our side of the river St Thomas' Hospital dominated the scene. This famous institution was first established in Southwark and run by Augustinian monks and nuns. It was described as old in 1215, so it has been there for well over 800 years.

Passing the hospital brought us to Westminster Bridge, which we walked under via the pedestrian underpass. Westminster Bridge opened in 1862, again replacing an earlier bridge on the site. It is painted predominantly green, to match, it is said, the benches in the House of Commons, just as Lambeth Bridge is painted red to match those in the House of Lords.

We rejoined the wide pathway along the river, immediately passing in front of County Hall. Once the home of the old Greater London Council, now it houses among other things the London Aquarium. It is an impressive building, but close up its elegance is lost. By now the walkway, known here as The Queen's Walk, was packed with tourists. We persevered, taking photographs when we could. For the first time we found walking difficult, as we tried to make our way through the crowds milling round the London Eye and watching the numerous street entertainers. The throng of tourists gradually thinned out a little as we neared Hungerford Bridge. This is a railway bridge, which takes the lines over to Charing Cross station. There is a comparatively new footbridge alongside it which allows pedestrians to cross the river. This is a marvellous viewpoint that takes in many of the landmarks of London. On the northern side of the river, the grand Victorian buildings along the Strand stand out, while on the South Bank the Royal Festival Hall and the Shell Centre dominate the landscape.

The Festival Hall is one of the permanent buildings erected for the 1951 Festival of Britain. Seeing it close up was a bit of a shock. I remember it from the 1960s as a modern and sedate concert hall. Today the lower floor has been transformed to house a number of gaudy tourist shops, blighting the appearance of the building. No doubt the concerts are still of the high quality of old, but the outward appearance of the building is far from what I feel a leading concert hall should look like.

We were now almost upon Waterloo Bridge. A modern structure with long graceful arches, it was opened in 1945 on the site of an earlier bridge. Nestling under its arches is the National Film Theatre. We both felt in need of a break and some refreshment, so we left the crowds and went into the restaurant there for soup and a roll. Unfortunately, I did not have my membership card with me to secure a discount.

Back on our walk again, we left Waterloo Bridge and continued along the wide walkway, passing the National Theatre and the Hayward Gallery. The crowds were still fairly thick, particularly around Gabriel's Wharf and the little area of shops there. Blackfriars Bridge, with its distinctive red and cream paint, was now ahead of us, and St Paul's and the City formed a distinctive backdrop. The present bridge was opened in 1869 by Queen Victoria and takes its name from the Dominican priory that once stood nearby.

Close to Blackfriars Bridge, and almost hidden by the throng of people when we were there, is the Doggett's Coat and Badge pub, named after an annual single sculls rowing race for apprentice watermen, a tradition dating back to 1715. A prestigious scarlet coat and badge are awarded to the winner.

An underpass for walkers below Blackfriars Bridge is interesting because the walls are decorated with scenes giving a little of the history of the bridge. As we left the underpass, a bit more of London's history appeared in the form of the crest of the old London, Chatham and Dover Railway, which used to cross the river here. The stumps of the old bridge that used to carry it still exist alongside the road bridge.

We were now in the area known as Bankside. There are splendid views across the river to the City from here, but right in front of us was the Founders Arms, a modern pub overlooking the river. At this time on a busy Saturday afternoon it was crowded with tourists, all eager to sample a bit of London life.

The pathway increases in width for a short distance in front of the old Bankside Power Station, with its distinctive central chimney. The architect was Sir Giles Gilbert Scott, who also designed Battersea Power Station. This imposing building was built in two stages between 1947 and 1963, and it started generating power for the first time in 1952. However, it had one problem: it was oil-fired, having been conceived when oil was cheap. With the rise in oil prices, it ceased generating power in 1981, and for a few years it looked as if the building would be demolished. It was reprieved when it became a home for the Tate Modern art collection.

Thames Path walkers who wish to visit St Paul's Cathedral, or tourists at St Paul's who wish to visit Tate Modern have a unique opportunity to cross the river here, because the Millennium Footbridge connects the two. This suspension bridge was first opened in the year 2000, but it immediately became known as the Wobbly Bridge. It had to be closed while modifications were carried out. Thankfully, today it no longer sways and it now carries hordes of people across the river.

Next we came to Cardinal's Wharf, where several old houses stand back from the river on a cobbled street. The 18th-century Provost's

Lodging, home of the Dean of Southwark Cathedral, is a little further on. Another house is alleged to have been the lodgings of Sir Christopher Wren when St Paul's was being built, but apparently doubt exists about the claim. Because of the crowds, it was impossible to take any photographs here, so we pressed on.

Walking along this stretch of the river, it is easy to understand why visitors flock to this area. There is so much to see, with every few yards producing a new view of London's history. Within yards of us now was one of the most famous. This is Shakespeare's Globe Theatre, a replica of the 16th-century playhouse that once stood nearby and was associated with William Shakespeare. The modern copy uses similar materials to the original. In Shakespeare's day this area was where most of the entertainment for the city took place. The City frowned on such low entertainment, so the playhouses, brothels and taverns adopted Bankside. Oddly enough, this area was under the jurisdiction of the Bishop of Winchester, who had a palace nearby.

A pub called The Swan at the Globe stands next to the Globe Theatre. On the day we passed it was almost impossible to get through the door because of all the people there.

The green and white Southwark Bridge is the next river crossing. It was opened in 1921 by King George V and Queen Mary. It links the City of London with Southwark for both vehicles and pedestrians. It has been said that it is the least-used bridge in central London.

Southwark Bridge is followed by Cannon Street Railway Bridge. Standing on a corner nearby is The Anchor, an interesting pub that has an old-world charm about it. There has been a pub on this site for hundreds of years. Samuel Pepys is reputed to have watched the Fire of London from here.

Walking past The Anchor brought us to Clink Street, a dark and dismal alley that is narrow and hemmed in by tall buildings. This is where the Clink prison once stood, from which comes the expression 'in the clink'. The alley is quite short and at its end reveals another piece of history: the remains of Winchester Palace, former residence of the Bishops of Winchester. Very little of the original building is still standing, but there is a striking example of a rose window.

Just a few yards away is St Mary Overie Dock, which contains a full-size replica of the *Golden Hinde,* the ship in which Sir Francis Drake circumnavigated the world between 1577 and 1580.

There is a Caffè Nero in the shadow of the *Golden Hinde*, but any thoughts of stopping here for refreshment were completely dashed, as the crowds seemed to be thicker than ever. We caught a glimpse of the Old Thameside Inn, which occupies a space on the riverside next to the *Golden Hinde*. It has to be said that it is certainly not old in appearance, but apparently it has some very good views of the river. This area is known as Pickfords Wharf, a reminder of the time when ships came up the river to unload goods.

Just a short walk from here brought us to an unexpected view. Surrounded by offices and the remains of warehouses is Southwark Cathedral. In previous times it was known as St Mary Overie, and this is how the dock that houses the *Golden Hinde* got its name. The guidebook told us that the cathedral has quite an impressive interior, but with the crowds still quite dense, we decided to postpone a visit to another day. There is a café adjoining the cathedral: another useful stop for Thames Path walkers in need of refreshment.

After Southwark Cathedral the Thames Path continues along a street with an interesting pub on the corner called The Mudlark. Mudlarks were small boys who searched the mud on the edge of the river for any useful items left by the receding tide.

The pub sign gives an excellent colourful example.

We followed the street to London Bridge, which is not a bridge that is popularly associated with London: quite often Tower Bridge is mistaken for it. There has been a crossing on the river here since Roman times, and over the centuries a number of bridges have been built at this spot. From medieval times there were houses and shops on the bridge, and the congestion became so great that in the eighteenth century a law was introduced by the Mayor of London, which stipulated that a 'keep left' rule had to be followed. Many people believe that is why we now drive on the left. The current bridge is quite a 'youngster': it was opened by Queen Elizabeth II in 1973. The Victorian bridge it replaced was sold to an American entrepreneur and was rebuilt in Lake Havasu City, Arizona. It has been claimed that the purchasers believed that they were buying Tower Bridge, but this is disputed and does not appear to be accurate.

We walked under the bridge and continued on our way. At the entrance to Tooley Street is London Bridge station, opened in 1836 and claimed to be one of the oldest railway stations in London, the one at Deptford having opened a few months earlier. On the opposite side of the road is London Bridge Hospital. We found Tooley Street as congested as the area around Clink Street. This is not surprising, because it has become popular with tourists since the opening of the London Dungeon and several other museums nearby. In addition there is a new shopping mall in one of the old dock buildings.

The Thames Path sign directed us back to the river and Hays Wharf. This area was once known as the Larder of London, because of the vast amount of food that was unloaded here from ships from all over the world. At one time, the Hays Company's activities extended from London Bridge to Tower Bridge. Today all the docks have gone and the warehouses have either been demolished or put to another use. An arcade of shops and restaurants called Hays Galleria now stands on the site, and we took the opportunity to walk through on our way back to the river. David Kemp's kinetic sculpture *The Navigators* is centre stage.

An impressive sight as we reached the riverfront was the cruiser HMS *Belfast*, which has been open as a museum since 1971. Launched in 1938, not only did she have an impressive World War II record, but she went on to serve in the Korean War, and was finally retired from active service in 1963. With Tower Bridge in the background, the scene had all the makings of a good photograph, had it been possible to take one. We had thought the crowds might have subsided by the time we left Tooley Street. However, this was not so: the area round the *Belfast* was teeming with people.

The end of our walk was now in sight. Tower Bridge was just ahead. We came to City Hall, opened in 2002, a modern spectacle of glass with a prime view over the Thames. Here, too, there were quite a few people, but nowhere near as many as we had previously encountered. The walk is also much wider on this part of the route.

It is only a short step from City Hall to Tower Bridge. If we had to choose just two objects that symbolise London to the rest of the world, one could be Big Ben and the other Tower Bridge. Both are easily recognisable the world over. Ever since it opened in 1894, Tower Bridge has stood majestically in its position close to its nearest rival, the Tower of London. Once it was kept busy opening to allow ships to pass through; now it enjoys a more leisurely life, providing interest for the thousands of tourists who flock to see it each year. It was late in the afternoon when we arrived. We climbed the steps to the bridge and waited for a bus at the crowded stop. Eventually one came along that was going our way, and we took our seats thankfully, tired after our busy day, but eager to view the city from a different angle.

There was a great feeling of satisfaction now. We had completed fourteen of the fifteen sections of the Thames Path, and now we could not wait to complete the walk to the Barrier, the finale of our journey.

Tower Bridge To The Thames Barrier (Southern Route)

10.2 MILES (16.4 KILOMETRES)

The end of our long walk was now in sight and we looked forward to it with anticipation and excitement. With a fine and sunny day forecast, we made another early start, and seven o'clock in the morning found us in Trafalgar Square, the nearest point the no.13 bus we had taken from Baker Street could deliver us to the river. After the crowds of people we had encountered on the previous section, we had decided to walk from the Festival Hall to Tower Bridge again and perhaps see things in more detail without having our view obscured most of the time. We made our way down Villiers Street to the Embankment, hoping to call in at Costa on the way for our early-morning coffee. To our dismay it did not open until eight o'clock. A bit of a shock, because when we had telephoned the previous day we had been told it would be open at half past seven. We decided to press on with the walk. The thought of waiting around for half an hour was not appealing.

As we were on the north side of the river, it was necessary to cross to the South Bank by using Hungerford Bridge. It was pleasant walking across the river, watching the sun start to warm up the scenery. There were few people around, either jogging or taking an early-morning stroll. We retraced our steps to Tower Bridge. This time, without the crowds, it was so much easier to take photographs and read the descriptive notices on the walls. One pleasant find in the shadow of the *Golden Hinde* was a Caffè Nero coffee shop – and it was open! We could not resist the opportunity offered, and the hot coffee and comfort stop restored our confidence in London's hospitality. The rear windows of the establishment overlooked the west gable of Winchester Palace, with its fine rose window. When we were outside again, I attempted to take a photograph in the rather bad lighting conditions. A workman spotting me stopped to say that if I wanted to wait half an hour the scaffolding against the wall would no longer be there. There would also be a viewing platform eventually, he advised me. I thanked him and told him I would be coming back another time.

We continued our walk, under London Bridge and into Tooley Street, then through the shopping piazza on Hays Wharf. Once again we passed City Hall with its view of HMS *Belfast* sitting calmly at its anchorage waiting for the hundreds of tourists who in a few hours' time would crowd its decks.

Tower Bridge loomed above us and we found the path beneath the road, passing the entrance to the engine house. Now we were on fresh territory. It had taken us over an hour and a half to retrace our steps of the previous week, as we had taken our time, but we agreed that it had been well worth the effort. Seeing the landmarks without the crowds had been a rewarding experience. We had been able to view the area in a completely different light, erasing our rather poor impression of the previous walk. This short section of the river is crammed with history and it demands a leisurely approach.

Leaving Tower Bridge brought us to Shad Thames. A rather odd name, possibly one of the best explanations being that it is an abbreviation for St John at Thames, referring to the area's association with the Knights Templar who were once established in the area. The street is lined with former warehouses, linked together at intervals with steel lattice bridges, originally constructed to facilitate the transfer of goods from one to another. Now all the buildings have been turned into apartments.

We did not dwell there long; the Thames Path sign pointed once again to the river.

A passageway with the intriguing name Maggie Blake's Cause brought us back to the river edge and the frontage of Butler's Wharf. We discovered that when the area was converted from warehouses, the developers wanted to restrict access to the river and exploit the area for commercial purposes. Thanks to Maggie Blake and other local activists this did not happen.

In its heyday Butler's Wharf was one of the biggest wharf areas on the Thames. Gone are the times when this part of the river was the heart of the docklands, the busy wharves lined with ships bringing goods from all over the world to be stored in the adjoining warehouses. Instead of warehouses, apartments and restaurants now occupy the area, and the bank of the Thames has been transformed into a pleasant promenade. Just after rejoining the river we came across a giant anchor on the walkway, and Eduardo Paolozzi's *Head of Invention*, a huge bronze sculpture of a human head lying on its side – both part of the refurbishment of the area. Close by is the building housing the Design Museum.

As Butler's Wharf ends, a footbridge takes the walker across St Saviour's Dock, a muddy inlet lined with warehouses, legacy from Victorian times, to New Concordia Wharf, once the site of a flour mill, which borders on Bermondsey Wall West. The guidebook tells us that this was once known as Jacob's Island, a notorious Victorian slum. Charles Dickens used it as a setting in *Oliver Twist*. For a short distance the trail follows a little lane and then leads into Chambers Street, followed soon afterwards by a left turn into Loftie Street.

Crossing Fountain Green Square, we found the riverside again. Across the river we could see a block of apartments with the name

Oliver's Wharf clearly readable. This warehouse was one of the first to be converted into dwellings and can still be clearly recognised from old photographs of the area. Now the pathway ahead of us was a broad walkway to Angel Wharf, with the old Angel pub close by. We almost missed a sculpture of a man sitting on a bench. This work by Diane Gorvin is a tribute to Doctor Salter, a local benefactor and MP in the 1920s. Close by on a grassed area are the remains of King Edward III's moated manor house, built in 1353 and recently rediscovered in the foundations of a warehouse.

A narrow passageway brought us to the 18th-century church of St Mary, Rotherhithe, the interior of which incorporates a good deal of ship's timber. A church had stood on this site for centuries before this. In 1620 the *Mayflower* sailed from Rotherhithe to Southampton in preparation for the historic voyage that would carry the Pilgrim Fathers to the New World. Christopher Jones, master of the vessel, is buried in St Mary's churchyard. Right opposite is the Mayflower pub, known as the Shippe at the time of the sailing.

Not far from the church is a building with a tall, iron-topped chimney. This is the engine house built by Marc Isambard Brunel (father of the better-known Isambard Kingdom Brunel) to drain the 1,300-foot (400-metre) Thames Tunnel he constructed under the river to connect Rotherhithe and Wapping. Although the tunnel was originally intended for horse-drawn traffic, it was never used for that purpose. It was opened to pedestrians in 1843 and today it takes the London Overground railway beneath the river. Rotherhithe station is close by. We noticed a sign on a wall that indicated '2 miles to London Bridge'.

The route now follows Rotherhithe Street for a short distance, and then returns to the river briefly. Here the walker comes upon a sculpture by Peter McLean with the fascinating title *SunbeamWeekly and the Pilgrim's Pocket*. A 1930s' lad reads the story of the *Mayflower*, unaware that a pilgrim is looking over his shoulder.

Points of interest come thick and fast now. After a brief return to

Rotherhithe Street we crossed the red lift bridge over the Surrey Water entry. A little later we came to Globe Wharf and the former rice mill, which blocks the way for a while and necessitates another detour to the road. The Rotherhithe Heritage Museum is here, in the old pumphouse that was built in 1929 to control the water level in Surrey Docks. Just beyond this is Lavender Pond Nature Park, a tiny area of marsh and meadow.

Back at the river, we walked along Sovereign View until Canada Wharf blocked the way; then it was another return to Rotherhithe Street, passing the Hilton London Docklands Riverside hotel on the way. Just after the apartments on Lawrence Wharf we had another glimpse of the river in a tiny park that led us onto Trinity Walk. Where this ends, it is back yet again to Rotherhithe Street.

It was pleasant walking, even along the quiet streets away from the river. Most of the people we saw seemed to be local residents, some of whom were happy to linger for a chat. We spoke to one young woman who showed great interest when we explained that we had almost completed our walk of the Thames Path. At one point we met another couple who were walking the trail in the opposite direction. They were from Brighton and told us that they were doing the walk in sections now and then, whenever they had the time. We stopped for at least ten minutes and exchanged experiences. They had actually stayed in one of the hotels we had enjoyed a glass of cider in earlier on our walk.

As Rotherhithe Street turns away from the river there is a rather pleasant surprise. Here on the banks of the Thames and surrounded by housing is a tiny working farm, complete with a variety of animals. Started in 1975, Surrey Docks Farm moved to its present two-acre site about ten years later and is now run by a charitable organisation as an educational resource. Sheep, goats, chickens and turkeys roam the small yard to the delight of the visitors. The look on tiny children's faces as the tame animals come up to greet them has to be seen to be appreciated. There is also a small café, and as it was fast approaching eleven, we decided to have a bowl of soup by way of lunch.

A back gate from the farm leads directly onto the river path on Barnards Wharf. Here there is another collection of animals, but these are cast in bronze. We stopped to chat to a young couple out for a walk in the morning sunshine with their young boys and seven-day-old baby.

Just before a big red crane on Commercial Wharf Pier, yet another diversion took us into Odessa Street, which skirts round New Caledonian Wharf and leads to the area once occupied by Randall's shipyard. This was alleged at one time to be the largest shipyard on the river. Suddenly we arrived at Greenland Dock. Once part of Surrey Commercial Docks, it now contains pleasure boats, and instead of warehouses, it is surrounded by apartment buildings. Crossing over the lock gates by the bridge took us to the lock-keeper's office and a return to the riverbank. We stopped to talk to a young man who, like us, was viewing the landscape of the river. It was very interesting for us that most of the people we had spoken to on our walk through London were not actually born and bred in the city.

Somewhere about here is the boundary between Rotherhithe and Deptford. It was close to here that a large naval dockyard was established during the reign of King Henry VIII. Now dwellings have replaced this, and the surname of Samuel Pepys, one-time Secretary to the Admiralty, has been given to the adjoining estate. The walkway ends at Pepys Park and at this point it is necessary to divert from the river. The exit from the park led us into Grove Street. A short walk down the street, and then we turned off into Sayes Court Park. The guidebook informed us that nearby stood Sayes Court, 17th-century residence of John Evelyn, diarist and keen gardener.

After following the pathway through the small, secluded park, we came out onto Prince Street. We walked to the end of the street, passing two pubs with rather interesting names: The Navy Arms and The Dog and Bell. Sadly, The Navy Arms was boarded up when we passed. When we reached the end of Prince Street, the directions told us to turn left into Watergate Street and then right into Borthwick Street; this eventually led us back to the water, passing on the way Deptford Green.

We crossed the bridge over Deptford Creek, the tidal reach of the river Ravensbourne, close to where it enters the Thames. Just before this we encountered a rather handsome statue of Peter the Great, which had been presented by the people of Russia to recall the time he spent in this part of the world. For many years there was an important naval dockyard and shipbuilding area at Deptford. Apparently the Tsar came to the area to study shipbuilding techniques and stayed at Sayes Court.

Leaving Deptford behind, it was now just a short walk along a busy road into Greenwich. We arrived there close to noon and found it bustling with visitors. Greenwich is a fascinating place. It still retains the atmosphere of its past links with the sea and seafaring folk, and there are numerous shops selling marine memorabilia. Many of the buildings bear traces of an elegant past. In the centre of the town is the 18th-century church of St Alfege, now sadly hemmed in by traffic. One famous landmark that at present is denied the onlooker is the clipper *Cutty Sark*. Fire almost destroyed the ship in 2007, but now fortunately it is being rebuilt, hidden from view under covers of polythene. Among the elegant buildings that perhaps symbolise Greenwich are those of the former Royal Naval College, facing the river as they have done for generations, with the magnificent backdrop of Greenwich Park and the Royal Observatory. Part of the complex is the National Maritime Museum, and this was our destination in Greenwich. It provided a welcome comfort stop, and the wide expanse of grass in front was the perfect spot for a leisurely break while we had something to eat and drink.

We spent an hour here before resuming our walk. We found our way back to the river and started out along the riverside once again. One interesting landmark on the waterfront is the Trafalgar Tavern, a popular venue with tourists. Here it is necessary to leave the river once again and walk down a narrow street, heading, it seems, in the direction of a dirty white building, which is the power station. At first it looks abandoned, like the other power stations we had passed on our route. However, the notice board told us that it was built in 1906 and that it is still in use. The Thames Path skirts round this obstacle and continues past the quaint almshouse of Trinity Hospital, established, the guidebook tells us, in 1613, by Henry Howard, Earl of Northampton. We noticed that the date on the building was 1616, but that may have been the completion date.

Soon we passed the Cutty Sark Tavern, an interesting Georgian building. Next was a rather impressive house, formerly the Harbour Master's office. Now as we walked alongside the Thames the industrial past of the area became quite apparent. Abandoned quaysides and jetties were in abundance, reflecting the time when this part of the Thames was a busy area for shipping. Ahead of us was the former Millennium Dome, built on the site of an old gasworks. The guidebook indicates that it is possible to walk round the Dome, perched as it is on a peninsula. Try as we might, we found it impossible to locate this route. The sign for the Thames Path took us into North Greenwich bus and Underground depot. We made several enquiries and were advised by a member of the staff there to go to the Thames Clipper terminal and find the way from there. After another unsuccessful attempt to find the route round the Dome, we resorted to this alternative path and easily found our way to the terminal, but in view of the time we had wasted we reluctantly decided to forego our circuit of the Dome. It has to be said that this part of the Thames Path is not very well marked, perhaps due to the huge amount of building work that has taken place and is still in progress. At present, the initiative is left to the walker, but no doubt this will change when things settle down. For us it was a bit disappointing, because we missed out on walking round the Dome and also seeing the giant cutaway section of a ship that rests there.

We managed to get on track again at the Clipper terminal. Great excitement washed over us now, as we could see the Barrier in the distance and it was a straight walk to it. It is rather pleasant along the route at this stage. Once again the path is almost like a promenade, with a bit of a seaside feel about everything, except that there are no crowds or children with buckets and spades. The Barrier became larger and larger as we approached. The end of the journey was now almost upon us.

Quite suddenly we were there. The Barrier stretched away across the river. A sense of achievement started to envelop us. All that we had experienced on our journey flooded back in an instant. This was what we had set out to do five months before. We had walked all those miles to be at this point of our journey, passing through varied scenery and watching the river grow in size. It was a memorable and precious moment. We lingered for quite a while taking photographs and perhaps subconsciously not wishing to leave the scene too soon.

Gradually our thoughts turned to more mundane matters. We had read somewhere that there was a café at the Barrier. It did not look as if we could enter this from the river, so we made a detour round the small complex and through the car park, which was strangely empty, and found the sign pointing to the café. When we arrived, it was nearly five in the afternoon and we were disappointed to discover that the café was closing. However, the friendly staff let us make a comfort stop. Johanna was still so elated that she could not help but relate to the staff our achievement. They became intrigued as Johanna went on to tell them that tomorrow would be her husband's birthday and that his first novel *Julie* had just been published. One young lady immediately exclaimed that as her mother's name was Julie and her birthday was imminent, she would buy the book as a present for her. Forward the author for another book signing!

When the excitement had died down, and without the availability of a coffee to top things off, we made tracks for home. From the Barrier building, we simply had to make the ten-minute walk to the main road, where we waited for a bus to take us on the first leg of our journey, and a quiet celebration of our achievement.

The Northern Route Through London

When the Thames Path reaches Teddington, the walker is faced with a choice. The marked path follows two routes through London: one along the north bank of the river and the other along the south. There are clear instructions in the guidebook for each route.

Initially we decided to walk the southern route, because we thought this would be the more interesting of the two. This is the one we concentrated on and completed in August 2009. However, towards the end of our walk we often looked across the river and thought that the northern route, too, would have its points of interest. In the end it became clear that we would walk this as well.

We commenced shortly after finishing the southern route to the Barrier and managed to complete all three sections of the northern route before winter set in.

We were glad we had made this decision, because the northern route has as many interesting features as its southern counterpart and is definitely worth the additional effort. We both felt that walking both sides of the Thames through London gave us an added perspective of this great river and the contribution it has made to the history and prosperity of the city. We thoroughly recommend that anyone who has followed one of the routes through London complete the extra three sections as well. They will be well rewarded for their undertaking.

Teddington to Putney (Northern Route)

14.2 MILES (22.7 KILOMETRES)

We were now in familiar territory when we arrived in Teddington. After our early start, we indulged in a pre-start and warm-up coffee, as there was a tinge of cool autumn in the air, though a fine day was forecast.

Half-past eight found us retracing our steps in the direction of Teddington Lock. However, before the lock we turned left down a suburban road clearly marked 'Thames Path'.

This road stretched for about a mile into Twickenham, with houses on both sides and not much else to see. It is also a main road, and even early on a Saturday morning quite a few cars were using it.

In Twickenham we looked for the Thames Path signs. The route is well marked and we easily picked up the right turn that took us back to our old friend the Thames. This was Thames-side Twickenham, with its desirable old houses by the river. A pub here rejoices in the quaint name of the Barmy Arms.

A footbridge from the river bank provides the only access to Eel Pie Island, once popular with our Victorian ancestors as a place to visit for the eel pies, until pollution devastated the eel population. The island is now home to a few permanent residents and some craft workshops. In the early morning it looked very quiet and peaceful, with just the odd person crossing the footbridge, shopping bag in hand.

We continued on this short stretch until the riverside walk came to an end. This was the interesting part of Twickenham. The parish church of St Mary's is a prominent feature. Some parts date back to the 18th century, but even those were built on the site of an older church. A visit is recommended, but so early in the morning and with a long march ahead of us, we restrained our interest to a photograph. We noticed the tiny Mary Wallace Theatre tucked away close to the church.

It looked as if the footpath might continue along the river here, as before us a tiny piece of open ground led to a wall with an open doorway. We decided to investigate and came across one of the surprises of the walk. We found ourselves in a large garden, and immediately we were presented with an unexpected and impressive water fountain. Among the rocks of the gigantic fountain, larger-than-life-size sculptures of naked ladies, straight out of Greek mythology, frolicked in the water. By accident we had stumbled upon the riverside garden of York House. Apparently the sculptures were purchased as a group in the early 1900s by a former owner of York House, Sir Ratan Tata, for the grand sum of £600. The house itself, once a minor stately home, is close by but hidden from view. When Sir Ratan died in 1918 his wife returned to India and sold the house, including the garden and statues, to Twickenham Urban District Council. The house is now used as the headquarters of Richmond Borough Council. Fortunately the fountain and the group known as The Naked Ladies now remain on view for the public.

Close by York House gardens is another interesting building. This is Dial House, which stands near the church. It was owned by the Twining family (of tea and coffee fame) from about 1722 until 1889 when it was given to the church to be used as a vicarage, as the old vicarage was in a state of disrepair. The huge sundial on one of the walls bears the date 1726.

Having exploited some of the interesting features of Twickenham with our cameras, we proceeded on our way, leaving York House garden and returning to the pleasant walled lane past Dial House, which leads to other interesting bits of scenery. The guidebook mentions a street of Georgian houses, and then, for those inclined to linger a while, Orleans House Gardens. Apparently a grand house once stood here, but most of it was demolished in the 1920s. The outbuildings and Octagon room are still standing, and these are now occupied by an art gallery.

Eventually the path took us back to the river and a view across to the opposite bank, where we had walked only a few weeks before. Somewhere hidden amongst the trees, we knew, must be Ham House. A sponsored run or something similar seemed to be taking place, because a crowd of runners were moving down the towpath under the direction of a tannoy speaker. On our side of the river Marble Hill House appeared in its parkland setting. We had viewed this from the opposite bank, and now we were able to take a closer look at it.

Richmond was now getting nearer. We could see Richmond Hill and the Star and Garter home perched high above the river. We passed the point where the guidebook indicates that Hammerton Ferry crosses the river for those wishing to switch banks or visit Ham House. Oddly, on every occasion that we have been down this way, we have never actually spotted it in operation.

Richmond Bridge was now in our path. It was just ten o'clock when we reached it. With memories of our previous walk, we crossed the bridge to Tide Tables café and sought out some refreshment. There were one or two people inside, but nobody taking advantage of the seating outside overlooking the river. The weather was still on the cool side and the fine sunny day we had hoped for had not yet materialised. Instead a covering of grey cloud prevented the sun from warming things up a little.

Invigorated by a hot drink, we retraced our steps over the bridge before using the traffic lights to cross the road at the end. The Thames

Path sign was pointing clearly down Ducks Walk. Perhaps at one time it was a common route for ducks, but now it is a road lined with houses. We followed it, admiring the dwellings on either side of us, until a railway bridge loomed up. Passing under it leads to a road bridge. This was followed by a third crossing, which turned out to be a footbridge giving access to Richmond Lock and the Old Deer Park, on the other side of the river.

Soon we were to have our first glimpse of Isleworth and Isleworth Ait, but before this the guidebook and signs directed us away from the river onto a main road. Then it was a case of following the directions in the guidebook and getting confirmation from the Thames Path signs. We crossed the Crane River, noted in the book, and passed the Nazareth Convent, another building mentioned.

We found our way to the bridge over the Duke of Northumberland's River, which is actually a branch of the Colne but retains the name because it was once owned by the duke. Eventually, after passing a pub with the interesting name of The London Apprentice, we found ourselves by the river again and in the midst of Old Isleworth with its older houses and All Saints' church. We had noticed this from the opposite bank on our previous walk. Sadly, the church was burnt down in 1943, not from enemy action during the war, but by two boys with a box of matches. It was rebuilt as a modern structure tacked onto the 14th-century tower. Like its neighbour Twickenham, Isleworth is full of interest and we were glad that it did not disappoint us.

The next part of the Thames Path goes through Syon Park. We left Old Isleworth and made our way up the road as the sign indicated. It did not take us long to reach the gates and twin lodges of the park. We found ourselves in a large open space with buildings in the far distance; clearly this was the direction in which we had to go, so we followed the path ahead of us. On our right was dense foliage, behind which, according to the map, lay Syon House, home of the Duke and Duchess of Northumberland. It came into view eventually, a large stone building behind railings. Syon House takes its name from the abbey that stood here until the Dissolution of the Monasteries in the 1530s. In the 18th century the first Duke of Northumberland commissioned Robert Adam and 'Capability' Brown to redesign the house and estate, and this is what we see today.

We wandered into the garden centre next to the Great Conservatory with its domed roof. There is an excellent café there, making it a good place for a stop on the Thames Path walk.

Leaving Syon Park, we found it necessary to once again study the guidebook closely and keep a sharp lookout for the Thames Path signs. Occasionally they can be a bit difficult to spot and two pairs of eyes are useful.

We were now on the edge of Brentford, and after a few minutes we reached the High Street. A turning off led to the Grand Union Canal. At one point we had some doubt whether we were following the trail correctly, but as the map clearly indicated that the path followed the canal, we ambled on, assuming we were going in the right direction. The towpath winds its way along the canal and eventually we came to the locks and knew that we were on the right track. The route is quite bitty here, but it is not unpleasant walking. We rejoined Brentford High Street for a while and then had difficulty finding the path back to the river. We made it eventually and ended up with a good view of the point where the canal joins the river. Again, this was an area we had studied with curiosity from the opposite bank and it was interesting to now explore it in more detail. It is hard to imagine nowadays how busy this area must have been perhaps a century ago. Then it would have been crowded with working boats carrying goods. The junction of the canal with the Thames provided an access route that runs 137 miles (220 kilometres) to Birmingham. It was a main artery between the south of England and the Midlands. Today it is just a peaceful little waterway peppered with pleasure craft and houseboats.

Leaving the area, we walked past some new apartments and ended up once again on Brentford High Street. Ahead of us now we could see the tower of Kew Bridge Steam Museum, but first we passed the Watermans Arts Centre. Apparently there is a café and bar here, useful for weary Thames Path walkers in need of refreshment, but on this occasion we did not investigate the facilities. Then it was back to the river and on to Kew Bridge.

This time we did not stop at Kew but continued on the Thames Path beside the river. Immediately after Kew Bridge is Strand on the Green, with its attractive railway bridge. This is truly a waterside community; with older houses set back overlooking the Thames. Dotted here and there are quaint pubs where the locals (and Thames Path walkers) can linger for a while over a drink and watch the activity on the river.

This pleasant interlude stopped after we walked under the railway bridge, because we had to leave the river yet again and move inland. There followed what seemed quite a long walk along suburban Hartington Road. It was another of those occasions when we began to question whether we were on the right track. Not until we returned briefly to the river did we feel reassured. The guidebook confirmed that we were where we should be.

A short walk along the riverbank brought us to a lock at the entrance to a yacht basin. We stopped and talked to a man we assumed was the lock-keeper, who told us a little bit about the area and pointed out the direction we should take, though this was quite obvious as there was only one way to go. We thanked him and continued across the gates, along Ibis Lane and back onto Hartington Road. The sun had been late to appear, but now it was a pleasant warm afternoon.

After passing what looked like playing fields, we came to a busy road. It did not look at all like part of the Thames Path. Appearances can be deceptive. Turning right as the guidebook instructed, we were soon at Chiswick Bridge, where steps lead down to the river again. Once again we had to thank David Sharp's guidebook for successfully navigating us through a diversion. We did meet people walking the

Thames Path without any form of guidebook and often wondered how they fared and how many times they got lost.

Back at the river, we found ourselves looking across to the other bank where we could see the old Mortlake brewery building again. The path now took us to Barnes Railway Bridge and here again was a brief detour away from the river. This time it was on a rather narrow road with sharp bends, which led past playing fields and, according to the map, to an area known as Duke's Hollow Nature Reserve. There was quite a bit of Saturday-afternoon local traffic on that narrow road and we were glad when we went through the tunnel under the railway bridge and eventually made our way back to the river.

Now it looked as if it would be a straight walk along the riverbank into Chiswick. In the short street leading up from the river we were surprised to find several interesting old houses. William Hogarth is buried in the churchyard of St Nicholas.

As we walked up the street, we felt inclined to stop a while and perhaps have some form of refreshment. Not seeing any suitable establishment in the immediate vicinity, we stopped to ask a young man who was helping his family into a car. He instructed us to turn left at the top of the road, where there was a pub. It was only a short walk and we found the building, a large Victorian establishment that seemed to be long past its prime. Nevertheless we went inside and had a glass of cider each.

It was close to three o'clock when we left the pub and returned to the Thames Path. The sun had disappeared behind clouds and the afternoon had become dull and grey. Our route now lay along the elegant stretch known as Chiswick Mall. We noticed that, had we waited until we were on this section, we would not have had to search for a pub: in amongst the desirable houses lining the route were several attractive ones with river views. Along the way, we passed the boundary between Chiswick and Hammersmith. At this point the road becomes Hammersmith Terrace. Here we saw a plaque commemorating Sir Alan

Herbert, the humorist, author and MP. Another, commemorating William Morris, is on Kelmscott House, Morris's London home, named after his country manor between Cricklade and Lechlade, which we had seen early on in our walk. The guidebook lists many attractions along this stretch and we thought it would be a good idea to walk this section again at a more leisurely pace and take time to examine everything in more detail.

Hammersmith Bridge appeared quite soon, and once past this landmark we spied Harrods Depository on the opposite bank. This time we managed to get quite a good photograph.

There were one or two diversions along the next stretch, including at Palace Wharf and The Crabtree Tavern, but these were minor inconveniences. The biggest venture inland was at Carven Cottage, where we were suddenly faced with the outside wall of Fulham Football Club. A sharp turn left took us alongside the wall of the stadium until we reached the road. Fortunately there was no home football match that afternoon. We walked past the front of the stadium and continued along the road for a short distance. After turning into a green area known as Bishops Park, we were soon back by the river. Somewhere in the trees on our left was Fulham Palace, residence of the bishops of London. Our route lay straight ahead to Putney Bridge, now in sight, where we would end this section of the northern route. There were quite a lot of people about now, many looking as if they had been shopping and were taking a short cut along the river home.

We reached the bridge and climbed the steps up to the road. The sun had returned as if to congratulate us on our achievement. It was late afternoon. We had walked since early in the morning, with just the odd stop here and there. We were thankful that we did not have to go far to find a bus stop: there was one close to the steps. An almost empty no. 74 bus soon came along. This would take us to Baker Street and a short walk to Marylebone Station, where we would catch the train for home after an interesting and satisfying day.

SECTION SEVENTEEN

Putney to Tower Bridge (Northern Route)

9.3 MILES (14.9 KILOMETRES)

For the next leg of the northern route through London, seven o'clock in the morning found us on the bus to Putney. It is quite fun riding these early buses. For a start the traffic is minimal, and on this occasion we had a bird's-eye view, from the upper deck, of London starting its working day.

Putney High Street was strangely quiet when the number 74 bus dropped us off almost opposite Costa. Though there was every sign of a sunny day ahead, the early morning definitely had an autumn chill about it, so we popped in for a coffee to warm us up before we started our walk.

Comfortable and refreshed, we made our way back over Putney Bridge to reach the northern bank of the river. The bridge was first built of wood in 1729 but it had to be replaced by the present structure in 1886, to a design by Sir Joseph Bazalgette. Sometimes it is claimed to be the only bridge in Britain with a church at each end: St Mary's in Putney, and All Saints' in Fulham. It is usually familiar to most people as the start of the annual Oxford and Cambridge boat race. It can get quite busy at times, but when we walked over it early on a Saturday morning the traffic was quite sparse.

Reaching the other end of the bridge, we took the steps down to the river's edge. The river was quiet and peaceful, with only the water birds providing any movement. We spent a few minutes taking photographs of the other side of the river and Putney Bridge from a different angle.

After walking along the riverside for five minutes, we found the way ahead blocked by the railway bridge that crosses the river. Now it was necessary to walk inland and follow several streets lined with Edwardian houses. Eventually the road ended at the entrance to Hurlingham House, which was closed to the public, so it was a case of turning sharp left and walking along Napier Avenue to make a detour round Hurlingham Park. Hurlingham House is a former 18th-century villa. For many years now it has been a sports club set in elegant surroundings.

Six or seven minutes' walking along quiet roads brought us to the part of Hurlingham Park that is open to the public. Here the instructions are to walk diagonally across the area of grass to a road that leads to the river. In our enthusiasm to get back to the Thames, we took off too big a chunk of land and ended up far away from the exit. It was a minor problem and it only took minutes to walk back and find the gate. This was a bit difficult to spot, but a kiddies' playing area gave us the clue.

As we walked along a road that had the intriguing name of Broomhouse Lane, we passed an interesting building in the form of a large house with distinct ambitions to be a castle. Apparently it was originally a school.

It did not take us long to reach the river again. A wide promenade stretched ahead of us with the river on one side and new apartments on the other. Tremendous development appears to have taken place along this section of the river. Blocks of apartments are in abundance. People who knew the area intimately sixty years ago would be astonished by the changes that have taken place to the landscape and the atmosphere of the river.

Wandsworth Bridge was now just ahead. We had to cross the approach road, which was quite busy with traffic. We used the pedestrian crossing and then followed the Thames Path sign that pointed down a road opposite. Once again we were walking away from the river, but only for a short duration. After making our way round the perimeter of the car park, we emerged into the more tranquil atmosphere of the river path. The sun was gaining strength now and the pullovers we had been wearing against the early-morning chill were now too warm to wear. We took advantage of a riverside bench to remove these and store them in our rucksacks.

The path led us to the area known as Imperial Wharf and the nearby Boulevard with its new shops and The Waterside pub, a picturesque spot for the residents of the nearby apartments to enjoy. Looking across the river now we had a good view of St Mary's church, Battersea, dwarfed by the high-rise buildings behind it. We stopped to take photographs with the aid of a zoom lens.

As we continued our walk, the big block of Lots Road Power Station loomed up ahead, bleak and abandoned, a sharp contrast to the area we had just walked through. The power station, which used to supply electricity to the London Underground, dates back to 1905 and closed in 2002.

Walking round the edge of the disused building, we were reminded of doing the same thing at Battersea Power Station on one of our earlier walks. It is a depressing sight, though plans are afoot to redevelop the site into shops and apartments. Close by is the muddy inlet of Chelsea Creek, which brings another tributary to the Thames. Somewhere we missed a sign and must have walked too far along the busy road. Using our instinctive navigation we headed for to the river, seeing a little of Chelsea on the way.

We were now back on the Embankment, in the fashionable area of Cheyne Walk. Walking along the Embankment is fine, but unfortunately the traffic cuts off any engagement with Cheyne Walk itself. Once the home of artists and writers, it is now only within the means of the wealthy. Well-known names associated with it include those of the painters Turner, Whistler and Rossetti and the writers George Eliot and Hilaire Belloc.

Close to Chelsea Old Church, facing the river, stands a statue of Sir Thomas More, who had one of the chapels rebuilt for his own private use. He was beheaded in 1535 because he disagreed with King Henry VIII over certain rather important matters of state. The church was badly damaged by bombing during World War II but was later restored.

There is another statue a bit further on. A naked lady stands unashamed on a plinth and oblivious to the traffic that thunders past. This is a bronze cast of Derwent Wood's 1907 sculpture of Atalanta. Not far away a boy on a dolphin tries to draw attention away from her. Yet another sculpture, this one is by David Wynne.

We walked on under Albert Bridge. Except for the constant flow of traffic along the Embankment it was quite pleasant walking. Fortunately, when our 19th-century forebears designed the Embankment, they included a nice wide pedestrian way along the river. The northern section runs for more than a mile through London, uninterrupted apart from at one or two points where walkers have to engage with traffic and use pedestrian crossings. Before areas like the Embankment were built, the Thames was a much wider river and places like Cheyne Walk were most likely riverside villages.

Not long after Albert Bridge, a green area across the busy road attracted our attention. A quick glance at the guidebook advised us that this was Chelsea Physic Garden or, to give the long title, the Botanic Gardens of the Worshipful Society of Apothecaries. Dating back to 1673, it is one of the oldest botanic gardens in England. It is open to the public in the afternoon, usually in the summer months. Unfortunately for us it was still before midday, so we could not avail ourselves of the tempting offer.

The whole vista of the Thames was now before us: ahead was

Chelsea Bridge, and across on the other bank the greenery of Battersea Park was easily recognisable. A few weeks ago we had walked through the park on our southern route. The river was seeing more activity now. Various types of boats frequently passed us, and the exotic yachts tied up to the jetties here and there gave a good impression of the river's new role as a place of recreation. Nevertheless, it appears to still play a minor commercial part, as some vessels that passed were clearly not pleasure craft.

As we approached Chelsea Bridge another patch of green opened up across the road. We knew we were now passing the grounds of the Royal Hospital, home of the Chelsea Pensioners, who are a familiar sight in the area. The establishment was founded by King Charles II in 1682 for the care of old and disabled soldiers. As if to give substance to our meagre local knowledge, one of the residents came into sight, seated on a bench ahead of us in his blue uniform. Chelsea Pensioners have an 'undress' or everyday uniform of blue, and the more familiar red coat that most people associate with them is reserved for ceremonial or special occasions. The resident looked up from his newspaper as we walked past, and we exchanged a friendly greeting with him.

At Chelsea Bridge we had to use the traffic lights to cross, as there is no underpass. Once on the other side we continued walking along the Embankment. Across the river was the empty shell of Battersea Power Station, its four chimneys reaching for the sky. It always looks such a sad building now, and we hope that eventually some practical use will be found for it.

Soon after walking under Victoria Railway Bridge we had an extremely short interlude in Pimlico Gardens, a small haven of green beside the river. Close to one of the entrances there is a statue of William Huskisson, who was a statesman during the time of the emerging railway system in England. It is rather sad that he is normally remembered as the first person in the country to be recorded as being killed in a railway accident. In 1830 he was knocked down by Stephenson's *Rocket* and fatally injured.

There is a brief return to the road pavement before an inconspicuous gate leads onto Crown Reach Riverside Walk, a narrow pathway that runs between buildings and the river. We stopped for a few minutes to watch the water birds foraging on the section of beach left by the receding tide. The pathway soon ended at Vauxhall Bridge, and here again some navigation of the road system was needed to get back onto the comparative peace and quiet of the Thames Path proper, beside the river.

Another garden shielded us from the traffic for a short while. This small patch of green contains several sculptures, including one by Henry Moore entitled *Locking Piece*. The Tate Gallery is close by, as is Millbank Tower, a 1960s' glass building.

We passed Lambeth Bridge, and ahead of us we could now see the Houses of Parliament and Big Ben. We walked through the gardens that separated us from the road. Across the river was the red brick building that we knew was Lambeth Palace. Closer to hand was an abundance of well-known landmarks, and the increase in people, mainly tourists, was evidence of this. There is an elaborate drinking fountain here, which the guidebook told us dates back to 1865, and as we left the gardens we passed Rodin's famous sculpture *The Burghers of Calais,* standing unnoticed by many of the passers-by. We took a photograph before joining the melee of people up ahead.

We emerged from the garden onto the pavement in front of the Houses of Parliament. In the small area surrounding the seat of parliament there is a great deal to visit and observe. The Jewel Tower, Westminster Abbey and St Margaret's Church are just a few of the 'must see' attractions. All were teeming with tourists as we passed. We had to almost push our way through the crowds in front of the Houses of Parliament. Making our way round the side of the buildings, dodging people busy taking photographs, we were thankful to reach the pedestrian crossing over the road carried by Westminster Bridge.

Once on the other side we were walking on the Victoria Embankment, with the statue of Queen Boudicca and her daughters in a chariot greeting us, and with an excellent view over the river to County Hall and, close to it, the London Eye. Across the road is the seat of power: the offices of Whitehall. Though the crowds had eased a little, the wide pavement was still very busy, and this situation continued for the rest of the journey. It was now well into the afternoon and possibly the peak time for visitors.

We walked on, taking photographs where we could. At Charing Cross Railway Bridge we came across an interesting reference to another piece of London's history. This is a bas-relief commemorating Sir Joseph Bazalgette, who in the 1850s solved the problem of London's Great Stink by sorting out the city's sewage problem. Until then all the sewage had run into the Thames, causing a terrible smell in summer. Bazalgette rectified the problem by digging underground sewers to carry the waste away from the city. At the same time, parts of the foreshore of the Thames were reclaimed and embankments created.

Once past Charing Cross Railway Bridge, we had a very good view of the Festival Hall on the South Bank, and then on our side of the river we came to Cleopatra's Needle, which was surrounded by tourists taking photographs. Brought by sea from Alexandria in 1878, the column has stood on the side of the Thames ever since. It is pockmarked by bomb splinters, not from World War II but from an early air raid in 1917.

Waterloo Bridge was the next on our route, and on our left appeared the impressive frontage of Somerset House. There has been a grand building with that name on the site since the 1500s, but the current one dates back to the late 18th century. Before the Embankment was built, the river came almost up to Somerset House.

The next item of interest is a pair of dragons that once adorned the Corn Exchange. Standing on either side of the road, they now mark the entrance to the City of London. Close by are the Middle and Inner Temple of the Inns of Court, another important part of London.

At Blackfriars Bridge we had to climb down some steps to a walkway called Paul's Walk. Here are toilets if a comfort stop is required. Across the river is Bankside and we could recognise points of interest we had passed a few weeks previously. The Globe Theatre was easily identifiable. We continued to Southwark Bridge. First we had to make a minor detour into Upper Thames Street and then quickly down a lane back to the river. There is a Wren church close by. This is St James Garlickhythe, rebuilt by Sir Christopher Wren in 1683 on the site of a much older church that was destroyed in the Great Fire of London. It features a rather nice gilt clock and was often referred to as 'Wren's Lantern' because of its many windows, built to fill the church with light. The odd name? It seems that it refers to a nearby landing place, or hythe, where in earlier times garlic was unloaded to be sold nearby.

There are some other interesting names along the route at this stage. Fruiterers Passage and Three Cranes Wharf are examples, each hinting at some of the history of the area.

After Cannon Street Railway Bridge, London Bridge was in sight, but before we reached it another landmark appeared. This was Fishmongers' Hall, the domain of the Worshipful Company of Fishmongers, which has been on this site since 1444.

We passed under London Bridge and onto an area called Grant's Quay Wharf. There is a gap in the office block and this gives a very good view of two London landmarks. One is the Wren church of St Magnus the Martyr and the other is the Monument, a tall column designed by Wren to commemorate the Great Fire of London, which started in nearby Pudding Lane in 1666.

Billingsgate Market is the next well-known building to appear. It stands almost next to the Custom House, where customs officers used to inspect goods. Predictably, the next quay we walked along was called

Custom House Quay, which leads on to Sugar Quay Walk, clearly another name from the past.

Quite suddenly we found ourselves at the Tower of London. Here it is necessary to walk inland a few yards and then walk along the front of the Tower, mingling with the visitors who have come to see this ancient building. This brought us to Tower Bridge, where this section of the walk ended. We made our way up onto the road and, tired but pleased with our achievement, waited for a bus that would take us in the right direction.

Now just one more section of our journey remained to be explored. With all our past experience, we now knew that when the time arrived for us to commence this final section, it would prove to be as stimulating and enjoyable as all those we had walked so far.

SECTION EIGHTEEN

Tower Bridge To Greenwich (Northern Route)

5.1 MILES (8.2 KILOMETRES)

We now had just one last short section of the Thames Path to walk. It would end in Greenwich, because there the northern route joins up with the southern one for the last few miles to the Barrier.

After we had completed the section from Putney to Tower Bridge, the weather conditions were not favourable for a few weekends. It was well into November before we were able to resume our walk.

Once again we opted to make an early start. This time the curtains of autumn had been drawn, and instead of beginning our journey in the light, we caught the train to London in darkness. It was still dark when we caught the no. 13 bus at Baker Street to take us down to the Strand. We had decided to walk a small section of the previous route, from Waterloo Bridge to Tower Bridge, again, before commencing the last section. There was method in our madness. For one thing, it was easier to catch a bus to the Strand and start walking there, and for another, we knew that there was an excellent early-morning coffee stop just across the Millennium Footbridge.

It was not even half past seven as we alighted from the bus and walked the short distance to the Embankment. There were now signs of light in the clouds over in the east. A fine sunny day was forecast, but this early in the morning there was a chill in the air and we were glad of the warmth from the pullovers we were wearing.

It felt strange walking along a deserted Embankment in the dark, brightened by the headlights of just a few passing cars. The two dragons announcing the entry to the City looked quite ghoulish in the poor light.

Brisk walking brought us to the Millennium Bridge. A few people out for an early-morning run jogged by. Already the sky was lightening fast, and the first signs of blue were appearing.

We reached Caffè Nero five minutes before eight. We spent a few minutes looking out over the river while we waited for the coffee shop to open. There is something unique and satisfying about seeing London just as it begins its day. It has been said that the city never sleeps: there is always some movement somewhere. But the feeling of watching it really come to life in the morning has to be experienced to be appreciated.

We were the first customers in the coffee shop and we were greeted in the usual friendly and efficient way by the staff. It was pleasant to sit over a coffee and watch the few first customers of the day come in. Most of them seemed to be out for a walk to buy a newspaper; others might have been workers stopping for a break. Certainly at this early hour of the morning there were no tourists. For Thames Path walkers, it is useful to know that at both Costa and Nero it is usually possible to make a comfort stop. We had learned early on in our journey the value of remembering where such facilities could be found.

Once we had refreshed ourselves, we continued on our journey: back across the Millennium Bridge and then along the towpath to Tower Bridge, walking now in daylight.

At Tower Bridge we started our walk proper. There is a walkway along most of the river at this point, with the occasional brief period inland, but even the detours are not without interest, often giving a glimpse of the area that existed when this was the heart of busy docklands. It is remarkable that, in spite of the development that has taken place, there is still a footpath along the river for the majority of the route to Greenwich.

As we left Tower Bridge and passed in front of the Thistle Tower Hotel, the first thing to greet us was a magnificent sculpture. This is David Wynne's *Girl with a Dolphin*. Close by is the sundial built by Wendy Taylor. We attempted to take photographs of both these items of interest.

Leaving these focal points we found ourselves walking across the entrance to St Katharine Docks, built in the 19th century and named after the hospital that once stood there. The hospital and over 1,200 houses were pulled down to make way for the dock. The docks themselves are almost hidden from the riverfront. The route led us along the aptly named St Katharine's Way for a short distance before returning us to the river again. This encounter was also brief, because the walkway soon returns to St Katharine's Way. Just before we turned inland, we had a good view across the river to Butler's Wharf, the first landmark on the river on the southern route after Tower Bridge. We could identify areas we had walked a few weeks before.

Soon we were in Wapping High Street, and not long afterwards we came to the small open space of Hermitage Riverside Memorial Garden, which commemorates the East Enders who died in World War II. We were now back on the riverside and passing apartment blocks overlooking the Thames. It is hard now to visualise what this area looked like fifty or sixty years ago, when warehouses lined the riverbank and ships tied up alongside. Only old photographs give any indication of the appearance of the working river, crowded with warehouses and shipping, giving employment to the thousands who lived in the area.

We had to return to Wapping High Street after a while. This is quite a peaceful walk because, contrary to what the name might suggest, there are no shops or supermarkets here: just dockland buildings mostly turned into apartments, all of them concealing the river from our view. We were conscious, though, that the river was just behind the buildings, particularly when we passed Wapping Pierhead, a row of elegant houses built for officials of the London Dock Company two hundred years ago. Close by is another well-known landmark, the Town of Ramsgate. This is an original docklands pub that looks out over the river. It has had several other names in its history, including Prince of Denmark and The Red Cow, the latter apparently named rather unkindly after a barmaid with red hair. The generally accepted explanation for the current name is that fishing boats from Ramsgate used to moor close by.

This is the area of Oliver's Wharf. It was here that one of the first conversions of warehouses into apartments took place. Looking at old photographs it is possible to identify exactly the buildings converted. On the other side of the High Street is Scandrett Street with, a little way down it, the church of St John's, Wapping, which used to be a landmark of the area in past times and has now been converted to office accommodation. Next to the church is the St John's Old School, founded in the 18th century. Above the doors are statues of pupils, dressed as they would have been in Georgian times.

Continuing our walk along Wapping High Street, we passed a rather inconspicuous building; only the police car standing outside and the blue sign on the wall identified it as Wapping Police Station, headquarters of the river police. They have been here a long time, keeping an eye on the river. The notice on the wall says that the station was founded in 1798.

A little further along the street is the Captain Kidd pub, another old Wapping alehouse, named after the pirate who was hanged at Execution Dock, close by, in 1701.

Our view of the river was still blocked, but we noticed that some of the names on the buildings we passed – Phoenix Wharf, Gun Wharf and New Crane Wharf – perhaps indicated something of their history. At one point a sign pointed back to the river and again we found ourselves overlooking the water and admiring the apartments towering above us with their magnificent view. We had to leave the river again at New Crane Steps, no doubt at one time an access point to the river between warehouses.

Turning a corner led us to Wapping Wall. As we walked along the relatively quiet street, we became aware of a coach moving slowly behind us and then overtaking us before stopping to park a short distance ahead. Tourists began to alight and disappear into a nearby building. We soon discovered that we had arrived at a famous pub and tourist attraction, the Prospect of Whitby, which dates back to the 16th century. It is said to be named after a ship from Whitby called the *Prospect*, which used to moor nearby, off Pelican Stairs. Because of its rather notorious clientele the pub was once known as the Devil's Tavern. The Thames Path sign pointed in the direction the tourists had taken. We walked along a passageway and had to make our way through a group of German tourists as they listened intently to their guide. Once past them we found ourselves in the comparative quiet of Prospect Wharf.

It was not long before we had to make another brief detour. After passing the entry to Shadwell Basin, we returned to the river at King Edward VII Memorial Park. Here there is a distinctive development of red brick apartments. We had noticed them from the opposite bank of the river and had been curious to see them close up. Nearby is a round brick building like a large tower. This is an air shaft for the Rotherhithe Tunnel; we had seen a similar one across the river in Rotherhithe.

The path eventually brought us to Limehouse Basin. According to the guidebooks, two other waterways emerge here: Regent's Canal, which leads to the Paddington arm of the Grand Union Canal, and Limehouse Cut, which connects to the River Lee Navigation. So it is possible to walk from here all the way to Birmingham or, somewhat closer, the Lee Valley. Perhaps ideas here for future walks?

The old dockmaster's house at Limehouse Basin has been turned into a gastropub, The Narrow, possibly named after Narrow Street, in which it stands. We continued for a short distance round Victoria Wharf and then followed the Thames Path signs past The Grapes, another Thames-side pub, which once served the dockers here. We read that at one stage of its life it was known as the Bunch of Grapes. The guidebooks tell us that it was built in 1720 on the site of an earlier pub, which may account for the plaque on the wall indicating 1583. Either way, it has witnessed quite a few changes in its history.

As we approached the Isle of Dogs, we pondered on the origin of the name. It seems that there are numerous possibilities. These range from the theory that this former area of marshland was once home to packs of wild dogs to the suggestion that during the reign of King Henry VIII hunting dogs were kept here. None, however, appears to have been confirmed by historical sources.

We were now surrounded by the lofty office blocks that symbolise Canary Wharf. We had watched them grow in the distance for quite a long time. At this point we either did not read the guidebook clearly or there was a Thames Path sign missing, because for a few minutes we were lost. A lot of building work is going on next to the river, and this may account for our problem. We had to negotiate quite a busy road before we saw a Thames Path sign. However, using our instincts we managed to find a way back to the river.

It was quite pleasant walking along the edge of the river in the warm autumn sunshine, with just a slight breeze in our faces. Perhaps it has always been windy here, because, according to the records, at one stage at least seven windmills, used to grind corn for bread, stood in this area. However, they did not survive far into the 19th century. The name Millwall, given to the docks here, probably refers to this historical background. Apparently a bank was constructed of earth and stone here to keep out the flood waters of the river so that the area inside could be cultivated. There does not appear to be any record of when this barrier was built.

After this brief spell beside the river, we had to make another detour inland and walk down a rather dull road lined with houses and a few shops: quite a busy little area, with local residents going about their Saturday-morning affairs. Just before the next Thames Path sign came into view, a rather interesting building appeared on the opposite side of the road. This is a very elaborately decorated brick Presbyterian chapel built, according to the guidebook, in 1856. It was emphatically worth a photograph.

On our return to the river, one of the next highlights we encountered was the spot where the *Great Eastern* was launched in 1858. Isambard Kingdom Brunel's massive ship was too long to move forwards out into the Thames, so it had to be launched sideways. The task was achieved only with great difficulty and after a number of unsuccessful attempts. Some heavy timbers on display here are believed to be part of the great vessel's building and launching programme. When shipbuilding ceased in this area it became known as Burrell's Wharf, after the manufacturer of paint colours that took over the site.

We were now close to Greenwich, which was just a bit further along on the opposite bank. We could make out quite clearly landmarks such as the Royal Naval College and the Royal Observatory. For the last bit of our walk we were back on a road. We passed The Ferry House, which claims to be the oldest pub on the Isle of Dogs. There used to be a ferry close by, as well as a railway station, but the ferry ceased operation when the Blackwall and Greenwich tunnels opened, and the railway station closed in the 1920s.

Without warning we reached Island Gardens. These really are gardens, alongside the river. They were laid down in 1895 and at the time must have been a welcome patch of green. From the riverside here there is a marvellous panorama of Greenwich opposite. At the edge of the gardens is a round, glass-domed building. This is the entrance to the Greenwich foot tunnel, opened in 1902 to enable residents of Greenwich to cross the river to work in the docks and shipyards in or near the Isle of Dogs. The cost of constructing the tunnel, which is 9 feet (2.7 metres) in diameter, 1,217 feet (370 metres) long, and runs 50 feet (15 metres) beneath the river, was £127,000.

This was to be our means of reaching Greenwich. There are lifts for the faint-hearted, but for those with the energy and the stamina a staircase leads down to the tunnel. We waited a few minutes for a lift and then as none appeared we opted to take the stairs, spiralling round and round to the bottom. At the bottom of the stairs the tunnel opened up in front of us. The walls are lined with glazed tiles and the tunnel slopes slightly downhill for half the distance, and then slightly up again. Quite a few people were using the tunnel. We reached the other end and, to prove that we could do it, we climbed the stairs to reach ground level.

It was early afternoon and Greenwich was congested with people. We made our way once again to the Maritime Museum for some refreshment. This time we looked for the restaurant that used to be attached to the museum. We searched in vain and upon enquiring were told that it had closed because an extension to the museum was being built, incorporating the space that it previously occupied. We drowned our sorrows with a cup of coffee from a nearby coffee bar.

This was a bit of an anticlimax, because we had planned to have a celebration meal in the restaurant. We had now steadfastly completed all the sections of the Thames Path and felt like congratulating ourselves on the feat. Nevertheless, circumstances could not dampen our feeling of satisfaction.

As we left the museum, we had an idea. Throughout our walk along the Thames through London, we had frequently seen the Thames Clipper river buses, speeding along and calling at recognised stops to pick up and drop off passengers. We had been thinking that it would be a pleasant experience to sample this method of travel sometime. As we left for home that day, we thought, why not today? What better way to travel back to central London? We walked to the Greenwich stop and purchased two tickets to the Embankment. An added bonus was the friendly man behind the grill telling us that, because we had travel cards, we would receive a third off the price. Almost as soon as we came to the pier the boat arrived and we found two seats right up at the front with a splendid view of where we were going. As we sat there watching the river roll by and viewing the riverside walks on either side, there could not have been a more fitting or pleasurable end to our long walk of the Thames Path.

Notes For Walkers

Our walk along the Thames Path started out as a kind of exercise to demonstrate that it was feasible for two people in their seventies to walk the 184 miles of the route. On one hand, we wanted to prove to ourselves that we could achieve such a feat, and on the other, to encourage others in similar circumstances to aspire to a comparable objective.

Along the way it was inevitable that we would amass knowledge gleaned the hard way and from experience. After a while we became conscious of how to save weight by keeping the items we carried in our rucksacks down to essentials. The following few notes are what we learned and we pass them on for the guidance of others who are contemplating walking the Thames Path.

1) Ensure that you are reasonably fit before considering extended exercise such as walking the Thames Path.

2) Build up slowly on the mileage you walk. Do a few short 'test walks' if long-distance walking is new to you.

3) Make sure someone else knows where you are going each day.

4) Buy a good guidebook. David Sharp's *The Thames Path* is an excellent one.

5) Always carry a mobile phone with you and make sure it is fully charged before you leave home.

6) Avoid dehydration. Always carry sufficient water with you, particularly in warm weather.

7) Carry some food with you, but avoid eating large meals on route.

8) Dress appropriately for the weather. Several thinner layers of clothing that can be added or discarded are better and more effective than one thick layer.

9) Always carry a lightweight rainjacket and waterproof overtrousers with you if possible.

10) Wear sensible boots or shoes. Parts of the Thames Path can be muddy and uneven. We met some walkers who were wearing high-heeled shoes or flip-flops. Such footwear can be a short cut to a sprained or broken ankle. For most of the route we wore boots or shoes made by Hotter and found their range of footwear excellent for the job. Ankle supports can be useful if you have weak ankles.

11) Check the weather forecast beforehand for the route you will be walking.

12) Carry a small first-aid kit.

13) Buy a rucksack that is comfortable, big enough for your needs, but not too big or bulky. An outside pocket for a water bottle is useful, and additional outside pockets are a must.

14) Take a digital camera to capture the scenes you come across.

15) Enjoy the experience!